WINGING IT

WINGING IT

A Memoir of Caring for
a Vengeful Parrot Who's
Determined to Kill Me

Jenny Gardiner

G

GALLERY BOOKS
New York London Toronto Sydney

Gallery Books

A Division of Simon & Schuster, Inc.
1230 Avenue of the Americas
New York, NY 10020

First Gallery Books hardcover edition March 2010

GALLERY BOOKS and colophon are trademarks of Simon & Schuster, Inc.

For information about special discounts for bulk purchases,
please contact Simon & Schuster Special Sales at 1–866–506–1949
or business@simonandschuster.com.

The Simon & Schuster Speakers Bureau can bring authors to your
live event. For more information or to book an event contact the
Simon & Schuster Speakers Bureau at 1–866–248–3049 or visit
our website at www.simonspeakers.com.

Designed by Jaime Putorti

Manufactured in the United States of America

10 9 8 7 6 5 4 3 2 1

Library of Congress Cataloging-in-Publication Data

Gardiner, Jenny, 1962–
    Winging it : a memoir of caring for a vengeful parrot who's determined to kill me /
by Jenny Gardiner.
        p.   cm.
ISBN 978-1-4391-5761-9
ISBN 978-1-4391-6899-8 (ebook)
1. African gray parrot—Biography.   I. Title.
    SF473.P3G37 2010
    636.6'8650929—dc22   2009040769

To Mark,
for a most original gift, one that poops thirty times a day;

To Scott, Kyle, Kendall, and Gillian,
for their always loving support;

And to Graycie,
who unwillingly gave up her flock to become a part of ours.

Contents

CONTENTS

Note to Readers

A warning on what you are about to read: this is a cautionary tale. By that I mean the reader might learn a thing or two we could have afforded to learn before we undertook parrothood. I hope one thing many readers will glean is that keeping a parrot as a pet is not necessarily advisable. Just as fluffy, buttery yellow chickies sound like a good idea at Easter but end up being fodder for Fido by the Fourth of July, stories about gregarious parrots might prompt a person to want one of their own. Trust me, think long and hard about this. I know that there is a tendency to jump at the idea, and the temptation will be mighty. But please, restrain yourself. Unless you're prepared for a lifetime of poop all over your floors, a coating of feather dust on your furniture, and the existence of a demanding wide-winged toddler for perhaps the next eighty years, run, don't walk, away from that pet store you're about to step foot in, in the hopes of acquiring your very own taloned television. Consider investing in a satellite dish instead.

WINGING IT

Feigning Julie Andrews, and Life with a Psycho Bird

If, way back when, someone had suggested to me that I would find myself playing a bizarre game of chicken repeatedly throughout each day for twenty-plus years, I'd have laughed and rolled my eyes.

But that was before a gangly, patchily feathered, and terrified baby African gray parrot plopped ungracefully into my neat little life. Despite its being the worst possible timing—tasked as my husband and I already were with a newborn—we took on the responsibility of raising not only a demanding parrot but a demanding *wild* parrot, which, at times, is akin to attempting to domesticate a rattlesnake.

It hasn't been all snake-charming, however. Sure, our parrot brought with her some unexpected challenges, but she's added plenty of laughter along with the angst and bird poop. This is the story of an unlikely alliance, of a creature who arrived at our doorstep by default. Like a stubborn adoptee who resents the family who chose to bring her into the fold, our parrot has taught us much about acceptance, about the importance of commitment, and, frankly, about how much bird excrement is tolerable on one's living room floor before it's time to get scrubbing.

～～～～

Let me give you a sense of what I mean by "playing chicken."

It's bedtime—the hour at which a mother tries to lure her children to bed, a task often met with resistance. In normal households, you might sing a lullaby to a petulant child to calm her down. So it's not a stretch to consider singing one to a petulant parrot.

Exhausted from a day of being a wife, a mom to three kids, and the one-in-charge of our two dogs, a cat, and a bird, I close up the house for the night, eager to go to sleep. The doors are locked, lights (nearly) out, kids in bed, but the most daunting task still awaits me. I wander to our parrot Graycie's cage and brace myself. She is happily ensconced on her very own tree, one that takes up some quite prominent real estate in the middle of our home and that we put there to appease an annoyingly intelligent bird completely bent on dissing us every which way to Sunday if she doesn't get what she wants. (Not that we let a bird control us. We'd be crazy to do that, right?)

My strategy—and there must be a strategy, in the interest of salvaging my digits—is thus: I extract the food and water bowls from the cage, rinse and fill them with fresh food and water, then replace them in the cage, hoping to lure her in with a meal. And then I gird my defenses: I butt the cage up to Graycie's special tree (her daytime residence) and tell her it's bedtime. Then I wait. If after a few minutes Graycie doesn't take the hint and meander on over to the cage—her de facto prison for the past two decades—I then have to tempt her. With *myself.* I tap on the cage, hoping the noise will lure her over. But often she's perfectly happy to just hang out on that tree, thank you very much. So I move on to plan C: I stick my fingers through the cage and wiggle them, making loud note of the fact that my finger decoy is there, like a human fishing lure taunting that elusive bass. Always, always, always, that does it. Graycie is off like a shot, moving toward me faster than a kid on the lunch line at a fat camp, hoping to take a fortuitous chomp out of my exposed flesh.

But I'm not one to let a tiny little bird—half my age, and I won't even go into how much less than my weight she might be—get the better of me. I retract my fingers. She's right there, awaiting my next move. As if engaged in a violent game of chess, I have to outwit her every maneuver, and this is the most important moment in the match: closing the cage.

Often I'll divert her attention to the other side of the cage by whistling her favorite tune, feigning indifference. I've learned over the years that my perceived indifference toward her breeds ambivalence toward me. This knowledge is a precious weapon in my arsenal. She lunges like a snake toward the side I'm on, and I quickly hop back to the other side, placing my two very vulnerable hands atop the cage, squeezing the metal openings together, and slamming the top down for the night, always careful not to crush her claws in the process. I manage this just in time for her to thrust herself back where I am, seemingly apparating from place to place faster than the speed of light, her beak jamming at every angle through the cage, hoping to get one more stab at me.

Cage safely closed, I can soon retreat to bed without yet again having to seek the omnipresent first aid kit.

But first, a little lullaby.

I toss the dark sheet atop the cage—this being the one thing that will encourage a comfortable sleep for Graycie and a good eight hours of peace for the rest of us. Then I lift up one side of the sheet, position my face up close to hers—but just out of pecking distance—and begin to sing:

So long, farewell, auf Wiedersehen, good night . . .

Julie Andrews I am not. But within two notes, Graycie's curious head is cocked my way. Her aggression has given way to enthusiasm. She tempts me, tipping her head forward and offering up the back of her feathered neck for a little scratch, among friends. I resist, knowing as I do that such a gesture could be intended as a bait-and-switch as much as it could be a charitable peace offering. I don't dare take her up on it. I continue singing:

I hate to go and leave this pretty sight
Do doodle do do do do do
Do doodle do do do do . . .

By the first "doodle" Graycie has joined in with her own "doodle doo," and we're singing in unison. The captor and the captive, the hunter and the hunted. You decide which is which. I continue:

So long, farewell, auf Wiedersehen, adieu
Adieu, adieu, to yieu and yieu and yieu

Do doodle do do do do do
Do doodle do do do do . . .

And now Graycie is bobbing her head, moving to the beat, thoroughly entranced with the tune. I can practically see her in a dirndl skirt, hands politely clasped, pin curls tight in her hair (make that feathers).

So long, farewell, Au'voir, auf Wiedersehen
I'd like to stay and taste my first champagne
Do doodle do do do do do
Do doodle do do do do . . .

Graycie is rubbing her head against the cage. *Come on, Jen, pet me,* she seems to say. She joins along, "singing" in murmured tones that sound like background din at a cocktail party.

I leave and heave a sigh and say goodbye—goodbye!
Do doodle do do do do do
Do doodle do do do do
I'm glad to go, I cannot tell a lie
I flit, I float, I fleetly flee, I fly
Do doodle do do do do do
Do doodle do do do do . . .

Finally, I can't help myself. I'm too tempted by the siren's lure. With apprehension I reach a finger toward the nape of her neck, ever so carefully proceeding to scratch. For a fleeting second I think she's going to relax and enjoy the gesture. But like a quick-tempered husband, apologizing for the backhand he's about to give his wife, she twists her head and clamps her beak down, so fleeting an action that anyone less savvy about her nature would have been instantly victimized, but I am prepared and pull back just as the bite is made. Thwarted, she seems disappointed. But I am gleeful and belt out the end of the song, knowing it also means I'm that much closer to my bedtime.

> *The sun has gone to bed and so must I*
> *So long, farewell, auf Wiedersehen, goodbye*
> *Goodbye, goodbye, goodbye*
> *Goodbye!*

I make a loud smooching sound with my lips, and she returns the audible kiss. I finish with "Say good night, Graycie. 'Good night, Graycie,' " my own little inside joke, a nod to comedian George Burns, then cover her up for the night, turning off the lights, both of us retreating to a peaceful slumber.

The crazy ritual is complete, and I head to bed with a sense of accomplishment, but knowing that tomorrow will bring with it more of the hunt.

And it does. Only this time, she gets me.

In the morning I greet Graycie in my usual way, speaking phrases with enough repetition in the hopes that she will pick them up (though I'm still waiting): "Good morning, Mr. Plumber! What up, homie bird? *Buon giorno, Graycie! Come estai lei? Bene? Benissimo? Ah, va bene.*" I have a thing for the Italian language. Plus, I'd rather she repeat these phrases than some of the more unsavory words she's heard uttered from my lips. As I open the cage, she's there. Bright-eyed, refreshed, and ready for volatility. Before I even have a chance to dodge her, she clamps down hard on my thumb.

The pain is deep and unmistakable, as if someone drilled into the bed of my thumbnail with a power tool while scooping out the other end with a razor-sharp melon baller.

Instinctively, I pull my thumb back quickly, enabling the completion of the bite, the chunk of flesh now missing from my thumb apparently lost to the bird's bloodlust for me.

"Sonofabitch!" I scream, grabbing a dish towel to stanch the stream of gushing blood.

I'm a serial curser on a good day and need only the bidding of some life trauma or stress to ratchet up the level of gutter talk to epic proportions.

Luckily only one of my three children is nearby to bear witness to this reactionary tantrum of mine. But then I realize the true error of my ways. My impulsively spewed invective is bad enough being belted out in front of an impressionable child. But it's worse still in the presence of an even more impressionable parrot with a gift for mimicry, who still, sixteen years later, is asking my once toddler daughter on a daily basis, "Kendall, do you want some strawberries?" A question the bird heard us ask our daughter occasionally when she was a year old.

Great. Not only did the bird achieve her perpetual goal—maiming with intent to injure permanently—but now I've upped the ante and given her a lovely little word to repeat to complete strangers for the next sixty years.

Sonofabitch.

I'm sure this less than blissful tableau has caused you to question: Why, oh why, would we subject ourselves to the crazy behavior of this parrot for so long? Why, too, would we be so cruel as to imprison a bird—the very symbol of freedom—in a brass cage? And why continue to tend to a creature that is at worst vicious, and at best entertaining but untrustworthy?

The short answer is because it's the right thing to do. We made a commitment to Graycie long ago. And to us, a commitment is a commitment, in good times and bad. Just like in any relationship between living creatures, things do not always go according to plan. But the right thing to do is to roll with it and do your best to work things through. Did we want to imprison a wild bird for her whole life? Of course not. But once here, she became our responsibility.

The longer answer is that Graycie is as much a part of us as we are of her. Sure, she might be feisty at times. But who isn't? Would you unload a grumpy grandpa just because he's prone to temperamental outbursts? Graycie knows us, she speaks to us, she's lonely when we're not home and happy in her own unique I-vant-to-suck-your-blood kind of way when we're in her company. Whether she's yelling at the dog or answering the phone or bobbing to the beat of the kids clapping for her amusement, she's one of us. Our parrot, petulant or not, is a member of our family for the long haul.

But how exactly did this all come about? How did we fall into the unexpected world of unplanned parrothood? Let's just say it was a bit like a couple deciding to no longer avoid getting pregnant, just to see where it would lead. We weren't exactly trying to become parrot owners, but we also weren't trying *not* to. To answer that question more fully, I suppose we have to refer to another song from *The Sound of Music:*

Let's start at the very beginning.
A very good place to start . . .

CHAPTER 1

The Man in the Yellow Hat

"Look. Don't blame *me* because you were kidnapped from the jungles of Africa."

This sounds like something the man in the yellow hat might say to Curious George. But in my case, it's a mantra. Something I repeat daily—sometimes ten, fifteen times—to Gracyie. In fact, it's a wonder she doesn't repeat it back to me.

Graycie has been a member of our family, albeit a reluctant one, for over nineteen years. She was a gift from my brother-in-law. A gift, I'm fond of saying, that keeps on giving.

Our African gray came to us at Christmas in 1990, shortly after we'd moved into our very first home in Springfield, Virginia, a bedroom community of Washington, D.C., four months after the birth of our first child, who was still waking every two to three hours at night, thereby assuring a personal mental incoherency unmatched since. This was back when we were still cloaked in the stupor of new parenthood, bleary-eyed and sleepless, unable to get a handle on one needy two-legged individual who counted upon us for virtually everything, and suddenly we found ourselves with yet another. Only this one had beady gray eyes, a beak that could snap my finger off, and a wingspan that would eventually extend a full eighteen inches.

It's not that we didn't want Graycie. We did. But as parents of a newborn, we were already wondering if we could trade in the exhausting baby for a pretrained child with good posture and even better manners. We couldn't deal with the parrot starter kit that would require multiple all-nighters for assembly: we wanted this sucker neat, sweet, and ready to tweet. We needed a maintenance-free bird—one that would regale us with its uncanny mimicry and not make too much of a mess. I realize now that this is like expecting a baby who never cries.

~~~~~~~

We probably owe our fascination with parrots to my husband's childhood in Rio de Janeiro. Scott lived with his sister Laurie, brother Mark, and parents Mia and Keith in Brazil for several years after his father's job took him to South America in the late 1960s. While there, Mark got a green Amazon parrot for his thirteenth birthday. Mengo was a beloved family pet whose untimely demise prompted Mark to stuff the thing and mount him so he could be perpetually remembered. Now we live in central Virginia, outside a small city that is surrounded by plenty of quiet countryside. Because of that rural influence and commensurate hunting culture, it's not at all uncommon to encounter all sorts of dead critters on display in folks' homes: deer, squirrels, rabbits, even the occasional bear. But I think I can safely assume that Mark's visitors routinely did a double take upon encountering the corpse of his soul-less parrot staring down at them from the wall of his D.C.-area home, back when the cadaver used to be on public display.

I suppose I came to the relationship with a modest interest in parrots thanks to my uncle Bill, who bred parrots years ago and had raised a stunning aquamarine-colored macaw from an egg. This parrot was imprinted from birth by my uncle, and despite his imposing size—macaws can grow to be a foot and a half long with a nearly four-foot wingspan—was an extraordinarily gentle creature. Billy took that bird with him everywhere: to the retail store he managed, on joyrides in his convertible, on the golf course. He loved it as if it was his child, and the bird reciprocated those feelings: Billy was its father, for all intents and purposes.

So perhaps when Scott and I ended up together, we were both just curious enough about parrots that it was inevitable that, with the help of one generous relative, a feathered friend (or foe) was in our future.

Scott and I met through mutual friends while undergraduates at Penn State. We were dating other people at the time and didn't start going out until we were both living in the D.C. area the year after we graduated. I was working on Capitol Hill as an assistant press secretary for a U.S. senator, and he was working for a federal government contractor for the Agency for International Development. Before we actually started dating, we'd run into each other at social functions all the time and say, "Hey, we should get together sometime!" But each time we set something up one or the other of us would cancel plans at the last minute. Such was the lifestyle of young professionals in D.C. When we finally got together we realized all we had in common; we couldn't figure out what took us so long.

Early on in our relationship I realized that Scott hailed from a pet-friendly family. When I encountered the menagerie of creatures at his parents' home, where he was living when we first started dating, it included two old and smelly golden retrievers and a couple of cats. Then I met his brother's latest venture in parrothood: some type of green Amazon parrot named Plato who had the personality of Sheetrock and entertained no plans of talking. Plato was best known for cowering and trembling in a corner of his cage. He did not talk, coo, growl, chirp, whistle, or sing. He simply existed. Oh, and crapped a lot.

Meanwhile, I was living with my sorority sister and good friend Tammy in Alexandria while working on the Hill. We had a fabulous time rooming together, occasionally threw amazing parties, and greatly enjoyed our yuppie lifestyle. But after over a year of dating it became apparent that it made more sense for me to move closer to Scott, who'd moved in with his two best friends in Arlington. When I wasn't at work, I was spending my free time at his place, and my costly condo rent on a very meager congressional staffer's salary didn't do my wallet any favors. It didn't take me long to relocate. I learned that a room had become available in a group house where Mark lived, just minutes from Scott's town house. The house was cozy, cheap, and a quick commute into the city, so I jumped at the chance to move in; once I became pseudo roommates with Scott's brother (he lived in the basement in a separate unit), I got to spend plenty of time around Mark's parrot.

Each morning as he left for work, Mark would turn on a parrot training tape for Plato's education/entertainment. Poor Plato got to listen to that tape, on which Mark had recorded two words on an endless loop, for hours. Even *I* got sick of hearing "pretty bird" as the words drifted up through the air ducts, and to this day I can still hear Mark's voice ringing in my head saying that mind-numbing phrase.

I'm fairly certain that Plato had been driven insane by the time he moved in with Scott and Mark's parents when Mark moved to Africa to work in the embassy in Zaire a couple of years later. And when Mark eventually got married, Plato—still alive, but without much of a life—was soon relegated to Mark's isolated upstairs office, where he was left to keep company with Mengo, high atop his death perch. Of course Mark was very fond of Plato, but after a while, what do you do with a scared bird who won't come out of his cage?

The icing on our parrot-shaped cake came a year or two later when Scott's parents celebrated their thirtieth anniversary by taking the family (by then Scott and I had married) to the Caribbean to sail on a hand-hewn schooner, skippered by a prototypically bearded captain named Ed and crewed by a sleek white cat and a yellow-naped parrot with the improbable name of Barnacle Bill, who did a damn good job of replacing a television in our lives during that week on the high seas.

No better or simpler amusement can be found than being in the company of a gregarious parrot. I think the sheer unexpectedness of conversation from a lipless creature enhances the entertainment factor. Barnacle Bill had the requisite parrot patter that any seagoing parrot worth his salt could say: *Yo, ho, ho and a bottle of rum, Polly wanna cracker,* and the like. But his repertoire reached far beyond the basics. He had us all in hysterics as he repeatedly sang "A Pirate's Life for Me" and the refrain from "So Long, Farewell" from *The Sound of Music,* complete with the *Doo-doodle-doo-doo-doo-doo-doo, doo-*

doodle-doo-doo-doo-doo. (I admit it. I filched the idea from Captain Ed.)

Captivated, we simply *had* to have a parrot. Scott and I were like young newlyweds upon seeing a tender baby sleeping peacefully in a mother's arms. "Oh, how sweet," we said. "We definitely need one!"

Those words would come back to haunt us. Upon returning from Mia and Keith's anniversary trip, I set out to buy my husband his very own parrot for his birthday. Back then, unsavory merchants conducted a steady trade in wild-caught parrots, and only the really ethical vendors went to the trouble of breeding parrots domestically (though unfortunately today parrot mills are common). Raising birds from eggs is tough work. In fact, not too long ago they could only determine the sex of birds surgically, so it was a bit of a project even to impregnate a parrot. Once hatched, infant birds have to be fed practically hourly by dropper. If you think a newborn *baby* is hard to keep alive, just think about nursing a scrawny, naked, defenseless little parrot.

So I researched the big purchase and found I could get an imported bird for roughly the price of a really expensive dinner out, which worked with my limited budget but not with my morals. I couldn't have it on my head that I'd contributed to the demise of a species, as these inexpensive birds were caught en masse by poachers who clear-cut trees in the jungle to get baby birds still in their nests. The mortality rate was high, as was the suffering: birds by the hundreds would be jammed into small crates with little food or water, ultimately bound for clueless consumers in the United States who, like us, wanted an amusing pet.

Well, I couldn't support that. I'd have no part in gratuitous cruelty for the sake of the almighty buck. Alas, there was no budget for a hand-raised parrot, which would cost roughly the same price as our week in the Caribbean.

So instead, we got a dog.

Unbeknownst to us, there was still to be a parrot in our future. Just not quite the type of parrot we had envisioned.

CHAPTER 2

Bird or Birden?

Just as a parrot is a poor substitute for a dog, so goes the corollary: a dog is an equally lame surrogate for a parrot. But Beau, a squirmy, frisky yellow Labrador puppy, was a welcome addition into our home and, with her many idiosyncrasies and even more medical issues, helped to break us into the world of needy pets, so having her was good preparation for what was to come. From her flea-ridden arrival (toxic dips being discouraged for young puppies, but for her insect-ridden body, a necessity) to her eventual diagnosis as allergic to the entire world, Beau and her commensurate maintenance regimen led us to *expect* to be needed by others. Not such a bad dope slap to two people who aspired to at some point have lots of children.

Around this time, Scott's brother moved to Africa for work. Fortunately for me, Mark's two-year tour in Zaire meant that I would be able to fulfill a lifelong desire—a trip to the heart of Africa. For as long as I could remember I had yearned to visit the continent—it seemed like such a mysterious, exotic place, and of course some of the world's most enticing animals were found there. Like many kids, when I was a child I entertained the idea of being a veterinarian. I was fascinated by animals, the more exotic the better. Some of the most amazing wild game on the planet lives in Africa; we couldn't *not* go visit.

So, soon after Beau's arrival in our family, Scott and I arranged for her to stay with my in-laws and packed our bags for the vacation of a lifetime. We arrived in Kinshasa, the capital of Zaire, late in the evening. Flying over neighboring Cameroon and seeing that the only light below us came from fires burning in the sprawling jungles—not a hint of light pollution to be found—was a reality check. The region appeared from above to be far more primitive than we had even expected, and once we were on the ground, we found it also to be imposing. Greeting us upon landing were deliberately intimidating gendarmes with oversize Russian machine guns and a combative Mark, who was unwilling to tolerate dictatorial bullying by a bunch of government henchmen shaking down foreigners, opting instead to mix it up with them in angry French while we cowered nearby, afraid and exhausted. We were happy to get to his apartment after a thorough grilling by bribe-seeking passport officials, who absconded with our passports for nearly an hour while we wondered if we would ever be able to leave the country.

By the time we got to Mark's apartment, which was in a nondescript high-rise located in an area of Kinshasa populated by expats, with lovely views of a lazy stretch of the Congo River, it was late and we were exhausted from travel. But we became alert pretty quickly when the first thing we heard as Mark unlocked his apartment door was a low, evil growl, a sound you might expect to hear just as a vampire has had his heart pierced by a silver stake.

"Holy shit, Mark. What was that?" I asked.

"Oh, that's Chaco," he answered nonchalantly.

"What's a shock-o?" Scott asked.

"Chaco is my new parrot."

As we flicked on the lights, we saw Chaco—a beautiful specimen of an African gray with sleek slate feathers that met with proud crimson plumage at the tail line, gray, scaly legs ending in sharp claws clutching the wooden perch on which he was poised, and a softer gray mask across his face with a jet black hooked bill that defined the word *threatening*. Chaco was without a doubt a dignified, regal bird—absolutely not needing the braggadocio rainbow feathers of a macaw. In researching parrots the previous year, Scott and I had read all about African grays: that they're highly intelligent and the best talkers in the parrot world. That as pets, they tend to stick with one person, shunning all others, even to the point of attacking what they view as their competition (oftentimes the spouse or offspring of the bird's owner). But we'd yet to see one in its understated glory. We were impressed.

And then it growled again.

"Hey, Chaco," Mark cooed, opening the cage and attempting to get the bird onto his hand. I backed away, expecting Chaco to rotate his head three hundred and sixty degrees while spewing green bile at us. Instead he pecked with malice at Mark's hand, which already bore wounds from previous attempts at making friends with Chaco.

"Nice bird," Scott said, laughing.

"It just takes some time," Mark insisted. "He'll come around."

More like he'd be soon repeating the word *redrum*.

Throughout our stay in Africa, I saw no improvement in

Chaco's attitude. There was no sign he was warming up to his captor, and we weren't scoring any popularity points with him, either. However, Mark didn't have to deal with Chaco's nuances as much as Mark's *domestique,* Bonaventure, did. That poor man—whose gig working odd jobs for Mark paid far more than anything else he could have gotten in Zaire—had the unlucky task of cleaning up after Chaco. This should have earned him hazard pay for having to reach in to clean the interior of the cage. Were it not for the man's twelve children, for whom he was fiscally responsible, I think Bonaventure would have hoofed it right out of Mark's place and never looked back.

Zaire—now the Democratic Republic of the Congo—was so exotic, a place where a talking bird seemed a natural complement. Even its capital was like no other city one could easily imagine—Kinshasa was a crazy cocktail of primitive and contemporary. There, modern high-rises housing the nation's elite dwarfed Dickensian scenes of desperately poor people cooking over campfires in the streets below while still others dragged their maimed, disease-ravaged bodies across lanes of traffic during rush hour.

Our first night out in the *cité,* as it was known, involved a packed, sweaty discotheque where we drank from the same beer bottles that we soon grew accustomed to seeing used to haul gasoline and motor oil along roadways throughout the country. (I hoped they were washed out before being refilled with beer at the production plant.) That night I made the mistake of consuming too much liquid, necessitating a bathroom visit. Too late I discovered that the bathroom was actually a very public communal hole in the ground surrounded by destitute street vendors selling Chiclets and cigarettes, a good two blocks from the disco. Upon realizing this, I cut off my beer consumption for the night and crossed my legs. I under-stand that much of the world relies upon this kind of archaic plumbing system, but that night I wasn't quite ready for it and the accompanying performance anxiety.

Our dining-out experience was equally eye opening. Wending our way past a decrepit elderly man cooking his meal on a sidewalk fire, we eventually entered a concrete building in the heart of the city and scaled two flights of steps to enter an elegant white-tableclothed restaurant for a fondue dinner. A big fan of fondue, at least the kind I'd expected, I was taken aback by the air inside the restaurant, which was thick with a cloying, nauseating aroma from the heavy, fetid palm oil that was used to cook the fondue instead of something more main-stream like peanut or vegetable oil. Turns out palm oil is pretty much the only oil used in a country where palms are plenti-ful and cheap, and I learned then and there that palm oil made me want to vomit. It didn't help that I have the sort of olfac-tory system that can detect a foul odor from thirty feet away— as a child it was my task to clean out the refrigerator because I could smell things just as they were turning bad. I resorted to plenty of that African beer to get my mind off the smell, once I ascertained there was a restroom *inside* the restaurant.

That night I never saw a strawberry, and certainly no melted chocolate. Instead we ingested a succession of gamey wild meats including monkey, elephant, crocodile, and boa constrictor (I was grateful African gray wasn't on the menu). Despite everyone's insistence to the contrary, none of it tasted like chicken, and unfortunately the gaminess would revisit us.

Back then I was quite the aerobics enthusiast and thus had buried deep within the bowels of my luggage a contra-band workout tape (Scott would've killed me had he known

I brought it because I swore I'd only pack essentials). I just couldn't imagine being cardio-free for nearly a month. So the morning after our regrettable fondue dinner, I slipped out of bed, donned my jog bra, shorts, and T-shirt, and began to sweat through my Jane Fonda Workout. As Bonaventure peered around the doorway at me like I was a madwoman, I noticed a particularly rank odor coming from . . . me. I was sweating out boa and crocodile, and it smelled like a combination of death and stinky shoes. From then on, despite my affinity for feathered animals, I figured it was a good idea to stick to chicken. And to probably not bother packing exercise gear for exotic vacations.

Our first road trip from Kinshasa was to Zongo Falls, a waterfall in the Bas-Congo region of the country that puts Niagara Falls to shame, both in terms of natural beauty and as a force of nature. Our drive to the falls occurred mostly on rugged unpaved roads with hip-deep ravines carved into them, the result of heavy downpours during the rainy season. The roads are not navigable without four-wheel drive, and not advisable without a bladder of cast iron. On the brief stretch of actual paved highway leading from Kinshasa, we saw many trucks, often piled high with more than thirty hitchhikers, who'd grabbed on to any piece of the vehicle available and clung for dear life. This was the country's makeshift public transit system.

On the treacherous dirt roads, we saw nary a sign of humanity except for a few villages populated by children with starvation-distended bellies and swarming with flies, hardworking mothers with tiny babies on their backs, and lazy men who sat around swilling banana beer and scaling palm trees, showing off for their visitors.

My brother-in-law had come prepared with a supply of American food we'd brought for him from the States (packed of course in Scott's luggage, since mine was already full of vital things like exercise videos). At one village—which consisted of a couple of clay huts, about forty people (mostly children), and a hostile stretch of sun-baked earth—we shared what we had with the waiflike children, many of whom were barely school-age and lugged younger siblings in slings across their backs. After videotaping and taking pictures of the children, who broke out into song and dance upon our arrival (we were clearly as unusual to them as they were to us), we distributed sticks of gum and pieces of candy, then tapped into the stash of "real" food from home and handed out fistfuls of Oreo cookies to our audience, fending off the men forcing small children out of the way for the treats.

Our destination, Zongo Falls, was enveloped in a lush jungle overrun with mysterious creatures, including tittering birds that sounded like wind chimes and chattering monkeys who refused to be seen. In retrospect, I think that Graycie would have been perfectly at home there. The falls, despite their powerful splendor, were virtually void of human presence. We happily—and foolishly—hopped from rock to rock atop the thundering water cascading down from the surrounding mountains to find a large boulder perched just feet away from the precipice. No "no trespassing" signs, no security guards to safeguard naive tourists, nothing but what existed a millennium ago and us—the perfect place to commune with nature and a couple of powerful Primus beers, awash in the dense spray mist buffeting off the rocks a hundred and eighty feet below.

After a while, despite my innate fear of premature death,

I agreed to join Scott and Mark on the lip of the falls, if only so I would not be the sole survivor if a flash flood suddenly whooshed them over the edge. I sure didn't want to be stranded in the middle of nowhere without either companions or car keys, mute when it came to Lingala, the local tongue.

Still, I was hesitant. "Uh, guys, *must* we?" I asked from the shoreline as Mark first boldly wandered along the jutting rocks leading to the precipice.

"Come on, Jen, don't be a weenie," Mark taunted. Mark has always liked to push me out of my comfort zone, even if it meant staying out into the middle of the night at bars rather than going to bed at eleven, as is my inclination. Or tempting fate by hovering over a waterfall. Next to him, my husband, to whom I'd been married only two years, was heading onto the rocks as well. Premature widow-dom was not on my agenda, so I figured I had to follow in case I needed to save him before he went over the falls.

"It's okay. Everything's fine," Scott said, reaching for my hand as I tentatively stepped out onto a rock, peering through a weathered hole in it roughly the circumference of my body as water rushed in a torrent just a foot or so beneath us. I would eventually learn that when my husband said this to me in Africa he didn't always actually mean it. Like when he found a grotesque, hirsute spider the size of my spread hand scurrying across my cot in our tent while on safari and pretended to discard it, even though he'd lost it in the blankets. Or when he learned—yet neglected to tell me—that the armed guards in our tented safari carried guns not to ward off the occasional *four-legged* predator but the not-so-infrequent (and gun-toting) *two-legged* kind.

Nevertheless, I appreciated their cajoling me, forcing me

far out of my comfort zone, and enabling me to experience life-affirming (or -defying, as the case may be) events despite my better judgment.

Our next road trip was to Goma, on the northern shore of Lake Kivu, and Bukavu, home of the Kahuzi-Biéga National Park, then sanctuary to one of few remaining populations of lowland mountain gorillas (now sadly decimated due to warring tribes in the region). We set off early on a gorilla trek, and not half an hour after our guides began to machete their way through dense vines, we happened upon a band of gravity-defying young gorillas dangling high up in the narrow tree branches. Moments later we stumbled upon the silverback leader, galumphing on hairy knuckles from thicket to thicket in search of tasty leaves. He humored us for a good thirty minutes as we discreetly trod through the near-impenetrable undergrowth trying to keep up with him. He seemed so easygoing, sprawled out like a fat, happy retiree on a poolside chaise longue in Palm Beach, stripping limbs bare and relishing the greenery he was ingesting.

We soon felt comfortable in his presence and were shocked when he'd had enough of his audience and elevated himself to six menacing feet tall, then stretched his seven-foot arm span wide and began to thump against his chest while barking out a powerful roar, warning us away. Allowing us no reaction time, he charged toward our group, freezing less than six feet away. Our guide quickly ordered us to avert our gaze, which indicates submission, and we stood frozen for several long minutes until the gorilla decided we'd been sufficiently warned and wandered off. The camcorder dangling from Scott's neck (he dropped it in the moment of panic) captured our nervous laughter and panting breath.

This world of extraordinary beauty yet imminent danger was Graycie's homeland, and having traveled a bit on Graycie's home turf, I felt even more remorseful that she got stuck living in Middle America (instead of the middle of Africa) than if I'd just rescued her from a pet store. Then again, the jungle terrain we explored during the trip—the environment in which Graycie truly belonged—was more hostile than I could have imagined. Remembering how frightened we were during our gorilla encounter, I wondered if maybe she was better off in the United States after all.

But the entire time we were in Zaire we never once saw a wild African gray. Or, I should say, we never saw an African gray in the wild. There was Chaco, of course, who was and would remain as wild as could be.

CHAPTER 3

Christmas in Shards and My Guttermouth Grandad

Upon our return to the States, we resolved yet again to obtain a domestically bred parrot. Sure, Chaco hadn't charmed us, but we figured Chaco had to be a one-off.

It wasn't meant to be, though, because parrots hadn't gotten any cheaper. Also, no sooner had I finished my recommended course of antimalarial drugs than I became pregnant with our son. Yet again, we tucked away our parrot ownership dream for another day.

Besides, having a high-maintenance dog was enough for us. By then we'd been working daily with Beau in the hopes that she'd become at least an approximation of a well-trained dog. Despite her being top of the class in obedience school, we couldn't even persuade our mischievous pooch to come in for bedtime at eleven o'clock—she far preferred to sit at the top of the steep hill behind our house and bark into the darkness. In fact, her bad behavior seemed to be on the rise, obedience classes be damned.

That Christmas was probably the last year of my life for which I was hyper-organized for a holiday, with all gifts wrapped and tucked beneath our tree weeks before December the 25th. As a sign of what was to come, I suppose, Beau helped herself to an early Christmas one night when we were out at the movies, by annihilating every last one of the gifts and polishing off a strand of outdoor Christmas lights—glass bulbs and all—for dessert.

We knew there was trouble afoot when our usually enthusiastic dog neglected to greet us at the door upon our return. Instead Beau cowered far from the entryway, feigning invisibility in the manner all dogs do when they know they've failed miserably in their mandate to behave. It was as if Beau were the sole remaining employee at an office Christmas party gone awry, left slumped in a corner, wearing a lampshade and no pants.

"Oh. My. God," I said after switching on the light, which revealed shattered glass and frayed green wiring everywhere but, curiously, not one drop of blood. We turned the corner past the front hall and found the detritus of what must've been one hell of a rampage, strewn across the living and dining room floors.

I leaned down and picked up several of our commemorative silver-plated White House Christmas ornaments—cherished annual gifts from our friend Paul—and noted they were mangled nearly beyond recognition.

"What kind of crazy beast eats metal?" I asked Scott. "She's gone mad! Do you think she's rabid or something?"

Scott just shook his head in amazement as he checked her mouth for cuts or glass splinters.

"No," he said. "I think she's ticked at us."

"Can you imagine what it must've been like to be a fly on the wall watching her go on this rampage?" I started to laugh, just trying to picture it, and Scott joined in.

We pulled out the vacuum and broom and dustpan and got to work, shaking our heads.

"I don't know what the dog had in mind. But we must not be giving her the attention she wants," Scott reasoned.

I just shook my head, but these words would haunt us for years to come, as the number of pets who would seem to demand an unnatural amount of focus, despite the fact that we both worked at home and spent much of our time in their midst, continued to grow. This problem was all the more frustrating since it seemed that everyone else's pets were perfectly content to just have a place to sleep and a few scoops of kibble, minus the animal drama with which we would become saddled.

Looking back, Beau's pre-Christmas antics actually seem like a walk in the park compared with the destruction our subsequent pets have been capable of. But this incident was momentous in that it established a way of dealing with such situations without which I'm not sure our marriage would have so easily survived: when the going gets tough, try to laugh, and then start cleaning up.

~~~~~

The next summer Kyle arrived, a nine-plus-pound watermelon of a child with a head elongated from a lengthy delivery, but healthy and happy nonetheless. Anyone who's ever welcomed a baby into their lives understands the tailspin into which one is inevitably thrown with the addition to the family.

The most basic of tasks become challenging simply because of the demands of a small being whose fundamental needs have to be met immediately or all hell will break loose. Kyle was an extremely agreeable, pleasant baby, except for his aversion to sleep. Everyone insisted he'd sleep like a champ due to his size, but everyone was wrong. Prior to his birth, my grandfather, usually a man of few words, had imparted his sage wisdom to me about child rearing.

"I have one bit of advice for you," he said as I sat in rapt attention. "Don't go tiptoeing around the goddamned house trying to be quiet for the baby. Let the baby get used to noises and he'll sleep."

Clearly I get my propensity for salty language honestly. But expletives aside, as a father of seven, surely he knew whereof he spoke. So I was intent on honoring his words. That is, until in our small split-level home every creak, bang, or bark meant the child woke with a wail.

My husband has worked at home for most of our marriage, running a design and licensing business. In those caveman days before we all communicated via computers, much of his business was conducted by phone, which rang all day, mocking my grandfather's reassurance that the baby would get used to all those household noises. Scott's home office was next to Kyle's bedroom, and each piercing ring of the phone or stomp of footsteps when his partner and best friend, Buddy, arrived and tromped up the steps woke our newborn son.

In those early days, Scott and I clashed over this frequently. I was so beyond sleep-deprived that rational thought and actions became a thing of my past. Not only was I waking to nurse the baby every two hours or so each night, but I was then getting no break by day. In the blink of an eye I transitioned from that blissful pamper-the-pregnant-mom phase to the blitzkrieg of bone-weary selfless motherhood, and I wasn't coping at my best. And as many new mothers experience, life as we once knew it for the new mom seems to be disgorged far more violently than it does for the dad, who at least can flee the twenty-four/seven baby demands at work. In Scott's defense, the emotional extremes imposed upon a hormonally compromised new mother are nigh impossible to reckon with. I was Tropical Storm Estrogen, and was battering down anyone who stood in my wake. And the more fanatical I became about imparting silence, desperate as I was for a break from the demands of babyhood, the more annoyed Scott became with what he thought were my unreasonable mandates.

To make matters worse, whenever Buddy arrived at our house for work, the dog would bark incessantly. The cacophony in our household was enough to prevent a cadaver from resting in peace. Woe to those door-to-door proselytizers who'd show up on bicycles in their black pants and short-sleeved white shirts, ringing my doorbell to try to convert me and waking the baby in the process. I probably came closer to converting a few of them back then, and not in a good way.

But within a few short months, even *hoping* for a moment of silence would become a thing of the past altogether.

~~~~~

That December, Mark arrived back in the States for a long holiday break and announced that he'd gotten parrots for the entire family (though Laurie's would arrive several months after ours). Scott and I were terribly excited, though this excitement was tempered with the knowledge that by then we were already in over our heads with the baby and the dog.

It's important to note that by this point Mark was on Chaco II, having realized that Chaco I was unredeemable as a pet. I briefly worried about the parrot's well-being before realizing that Chaco was probably the rare creature that was surviving quite well after being reintroduced into the wild despite his little stint of domesticity. That bird was tough. In any case, that knowledge, coupled with the vague details Mark offered about our soon-to-arrive pets as we exchanged gifts on Christmas day at Scott's parents' house, made me even more uneasy.

"So, your parrots are going to be in quarantine for the next several weeks, but I can tell you a little bit about them. Mom, Dad, the bird I got for you is a beautiful gray with shiny red tail feathers," Mark said proudly. He paused, then turned to Scott and me and said, "Scott, Jenny, yours has had a little problem with feather plucking."

"You mean it doesn't have feathers?" Scott asked.

"Well, it has some. Just not as many as it should."

Mark then turned back to Scott's parents. "Mom, Dad, I've been able to hand-train your parrot, and he's very gentle and won't bite." He looked at Scott and me again. "Scott, Jenny, well, your bird will take a bit more work."

"You mean it won't go on your hand?" I asked.

Mark chuckled. "Well, not without biting. You'll just need to spend a lot of time with him."

Perfect! Precisely what new parents have in spades: spare time.

Mark wasn't done. "Mom, Dad, your bird has been able to learn a number of words and loves to sing."

Scott and I pretty much knew what was coming.

"Scott, Jenny, uh, so far your bird just growls."

By then, I was convinced that Mark had gotten Chaco I off his back by delivering him to us. This was going to be marvelous. We'd just been gifted a parrot possessed by demons. Just what we needed.

~~~~~~~

We had a brief gestational period in which to prepare for Graycie. Much to our chagrin, Kyle did not suddenly choose to sleep for extended periods of time, but instead continued to wake up all night long. But we did find time to purchase a large cage and some toys, and scout out the area of the house most likely to accommodate a five-foot-tall cage, which ended up in our tiny but cozy basement family room. It was kind of like getting ready for a newborn all over again.

As we prepared for the parrot's arrival, we struggled to come up with names for it even though we weren't sure of its sex, though due to its smaller size Mark thought it was a female. Based purely upon its lackluster initial description, I started jokingly calling it "the Dud." As uncharitable as it was, it seemed somewhat on the mark. We ultimately decided to delay naming it, pending a thorough assessment of its personality.

Finally the Dud came out of quarantine. Quarantine, for the uninitiated, is a period of time in which birds are kept prisoners of the United States government (a sort of birdie Gitmo, without any Koran-flushing), pending disease clearance. If the bird dies during that captive period, the official government position seems to be that they were probably a menace to society—or perhaps enemy combatants—so good riddance.

Luckily for us (depending on whether you're a glass-half-full person, like Scott, or a glass-half-empty person, of which Scott has occasionally accused me, though I prefer to say he's the idealist and I'm the realist), Graycie survived prison camp in good health but bad temperament, somewhat balding and gangly—looking no doubt like a refugee. Scott and his father picked up the parrots at the Port of Baltimore, and Graycie arrived home to much fanfare: Beau went crazy. She was, after all, a bird dog. And it wouldn't be long until we discovered how lucky we were that Labradors have soft mouths.

The first sounds that Graycie made were familiar ones. A combination of Damien, from *The Omen,* with a soupçon of Regan from *The Exorcist,* and a dash or two of Freddy Kruger just as he slashed into his next victim, thrown in for good measure. A charming sound to hear when you're alone in the house at night. Our first babysitter, who at least was there during the daytime, taught us that we should warn people about our new pet lest they assume a demon was indeed haunting our house. This was during the days before cell phones, and we had arranged to check in with her periodically by pay phone. When Scott called home, the sitter sounded anxious.

"Uh, Mr. Gardiner. The baby's fine, but I'm hearing scary sounds, like there's an angry man in your basement."

Scott quickly explained the source of the sound, but we were lucky the house wasn't surrounded by a dragnet of police by the time we got home.

~~~~~

Early on, our other pets took to Graycie. Well, took to her as in she fascinated them and brought out a new side of them—

their repressed wild side. Our cats, Mink and Hobbes, who had both been declawed (one of those mistakes we always regretted but had done at the behest of a vet after a furniture-shredding rampage), weren't as much of a worry, even if they did regularly stretch their lithe bodies as high up the cage as possible to reach for the bird. Instinct, I guess. But they were basically harmless, despite the fact that many a time we found them nose to beak with Graycie, like the Russians and the Americans in the Cold War, each waiting for the other to blink first.

The dog, however, was another story altogether. We trusted implicitly that Beau understood that the bird was a family member, until the day we found her running around with Graycie softly nestled within the confines of her jaw.

We'd had Graycie only a few weeks when it happened. In typical Labrador style, Beau was thrilled with her catch and raced over to show us what she'd found. As soon as we discovered the dog's appetite for our parrot, we pinned Beau down and pried her gentle chops open, trying to free our already psychologically scarred bird. Meanwhile the parrot reached and strained to peck at her liberators—an early harbinger of her eventual lack of appreciation for our efforts. But truth be told, I could hardly blame her for resenting us. We were the enemy, and somehow we were going to have to prove to her that we were on her side.

CHAPTER 4

Are You My Mother?

So there we were, the real-life equivalents of the gigantic steam shovel from P. D. Eastman's children's book *Are You My Mother?* Only we couldn't put the baby bird back up into the nest in the tall tree, because that tree got whacked down to steal the baby bird, and that mother was long gone.

Sometimes I feel guilty about this. Deep down I feel like I've had my hand in the animal slave trade. Yet we wanted our very own African gray parrot on some level, at least in a theoretical sense; we'd never really implemented the reality check on the concept. And then suddenly we'd had one flutter right down into our laps.

I certainly would never fault my brother-in-law for his thoughtful gift, because twenty years ago, bringing a parrot back home while living overseas fell into the same category as parents tossing their kids in the back of the station wagon without seat belts for long road trips. We were all a bit more ignorant back then and were guilty of all sorts of minor sins we'd never commit now.

Suffice it to say that along with our bird came a certain level of guilt. But the fact was, we became our parrot's de facto mother, and mean or not, our little birdie was a sad, lonely creature. It was our responsibility to take care of our new charge and provide as good a life as we could, short of importing from Zaire some token palm trees and a few monkeys and snakes to reconstruct a jungle atmosphere in our humble abode.

About that humble home: free space was tough to come by when Graycie arrived. Putting a birdcage in the living room was out of the question—much of one wall was already taken up by my brother-in-law's loaner fish tank, which he'd left in our charge when he went to Africa. (It would be a while before he realized we weren't cut out for tending to fish any more than we were for a parrot; tropical fish went belly-up at an alarming rate in our house. We had far more floaters than swimmers within a few short months of his departure.) The rest was taken up by furniture, so we decided to put the birdcage in the basement family room. This was mistake number one: as we'd learn, jungle birds apparently don't take well to dark rooms with minimal natural light.

In the beginning, Graycie greeted us with those familiar Damien-like noises whenever we went near her cage. Our little bird emitted sounds like the last dying gasps of a broken-down jalopy with transmission problems, and the poor thing looked like she'd just been sprung from Ellis Island, in the same mangy outfit in which she'd left the homeland. She definitely fell into the category of huddled masses, what with her scraggly gray feathers looking like a frayed blanket, as if the bird had a permanent case of bed head.

She usually cowered, trembling, in a corner of the cage,

randomly plucking at her downy feathers, fearful of the toys we'd selected for her, and was happy only when peanuts were placed in her food bowl. These peanuts—which we were told were like birdie crack—are extremely unhealthful for a parrot's diet, and were to be given sparingly. But just like parents who are inclined to bribe their kid with ice cream or chips on occasion, we ignored that warning—we'd do anything to encourage her to like us. Eventually, though, we were chastised by our veterinarian, who told us the peanuts would lead to hardening arteries and a dead bird, and since we were determined to provide a good life for the Dud, peanuts were off the menu. Mostly.

This same veterinarian was our lifeline in those early days with a foreign entity under our tutelage. Dr. Stahl, a young, boyishly handsome exotic-animal veterinarian, was enormously supportive and enthusiastic about Graycie's potential, even when we called constantly with burning—and rank amateur—questions.

"She's chewing on her feathers. What should we do?"

"She's bleeding again. What should we do?"

"The dog tried to eat her. What should we do?"

For all our anxiety about handling Graycie, the vet constantly reassured us and injected some calm into our daily parrot frenzy. In fact, his enthusiasm for parrots was infectious.

"Oh, she's a gorgeous gray," he said when he first met her, stroking her feathers and holding her with no noticeable fear. "You're going to love having her in your family."

And despite her surliness, he remained upbeat.

"You'll get through this. Really, you will. She's young; she'll start to trust you and you'll be holding her in no time."

Dr. Stahl's excellent bedside manner was especially helpful when Graycie proved to be a bleeder. As Mark had warned us that Christmas Day, Graycie was a feather plucker. This is not uncommon in wild birds trapped in captivity. Just as a nervous child might gnaw her fingernails to the quick, so, too, an anxious bird will chew and pluck at delicate feathers until they are reduced to stubbles. The problem was, if she managed to pull out the blood feathers—the nascent feathers that erupt in a molting bird—she was in danger of bleeding to death. And Graycie had a penchant for plucking out blood feathers.

When a bird molts—or sheds old feathers, to be replaced by fresh ones—blood feathers are the replacements. Growth of these feathers comes with a healthy dose of blood flow, and with larger feathers, such as on wings or tails, the blood flow through the feather quill is fairly substantial; the shaft is almost like an artery through which blood streams. Thus, severing that artery by either biting the feather off or plucking it out entirely leads to bleeding. And unless the flow of blood is stanched, it could result in a dangerous amount of blood lost.

Suffice it to say we were lucky the room in which Graycie resided had ugly coffee-brown carpeting that hid most stains, because otherwise our family room would have looked like a crime scene. As it was, the walls got spattered with blood on a regular basis, and I learned early on that anything less than really freshly splattered blood is almost impossible to scrub off of absorbent drywall. We should've simply painted the walls a high-gloss crimson, or acted as if our parrot was actually our very own precocious Jackson Pollock type who artistically speckled our walls.

The key was to stop the blood flow before it became extreme. Which would be hard enough with, say, a squirming human being, but with a strong-for-her-size bird writhing in fury at being held down, it was all the more challenging. A veterinarian might cauterize a site bleeding from a plucked blood feather with a silver nitrate stick (an instrument that looks like a long wooden matchstick)—one or two touches to the site and the area would be chemically burned shut—but at home we were left to our own devices. Luckily we learned that you could clot the site with all-purpose flour. The stuff glued the boo-boo right up. Of course what usually happened as we tried to gum up the latest injury with flour was that the bird would break free and flap her wings in a desperate frenzy, and flour (and more blood) would scatter for ten feet in either direction. This would leave me with not just blood clean-up, but flour clean-up to boot.

Did I mention that we also had a small child to whom we needed to tend?

The bleeding happened on a pretty regular basis. Our vet felt certain that eventually our parrot would acclimate to her new life and dispense with the feather plucking, and we were hopeful about this. But we also weren't seeing much sign of improvement. Each time I'd find yet another blood feather at the bottom of the cage in the morning, my heart would sink. I fully expected one day to wake up and find the bird belly-up (or beak-down) and was relieved each morning when I was greeted by her menacing growl instead.

In addition to schooling us in the perils of feather plucking, the vet also taught us important lessons on parrot maintenance, like claw trimming. In the wild, a parrot's claws wear down with usage. In a cage, not so much. Now Graycie's claws, if left untrimmed, soon develop the fine point of a candy cane a child has sucked on for about ten hours. Only they're not at all likely to break before inflicting injury on whoever has contact with them. Those suckers are sharp enough to pierce ears. So holding Graycie is downright treacherous without regular claw trimming. Many a time I've tried to hold the bird, only for her to clutch my arm tightly so she doesn't fall off; the tighter she grips, the more the pincers sink into my vulnerable flesh. It reminds me of some sort of mystical eastern religious practice where you try to endure as much pain as possible, perhaps by lying on a bed of nails and having an elephant sit on you, or walking across hot coals despite your rapidly searing epidermis. It's that comfortable.

So every few weeks we have to coerce her out of the cage and then finagle her into a protective belly-up (thus undesirably vulnerable) hold so that we don't hurt her and she doesn't hurt us. Once we have her in the proscribed grip—thumb and pointer finger circled around her head, meeting at the base of her beak in such a way that it doesn't choke the bird but holds her head still in order for us to tend to her needs without exposing ourselves to bodily harm—we then have to clip claws.

I've had enough experience clipping animals' claws over the years to know that I don't like doing it with anything that snips them. Those instruments make it far too easy to get down to the quick, and that hurts an animal. Plus there is the added danger with a parrot that if you trim too far, the straw factor comes into play: much like blood feathers, birdie claws are conduits for blood flow. So we have to have a bowl of kitchen flour at the ready when it's time for a trim. We use a high-speed rotary Dremel for the filing, which probably scares the crap out of her, but which works quickly and effectively. The whole thing is a delicate tap dance as we try to keep her claws separated, especially as she is inclined to clench them, particularly over my own digits, puncturing my flesh with her candy cane points.

This, of course, is a two-person operation. At first Scott undertook the role of trimmer, while I was tasked with holding the parrot. I was none too comfortable in this position.

"I'm worried I'm gonna accidentally strangle her," I'd say to him.

"No you won't. Just be careful," Scott reassured me.

"I *am* being careful!"

Although that was easier said than done with a raging raptor (of sorts) in my hands. I'd try to stroke her tummy during the trimming to soothe her, the only time I'd dare attempt such a maneuver; I think she liked it. But this meant my hold on her overall was compromised, and then she'd struggle to attack Scott's hands.

"You've got to have a strong grasp of her or she's going to maul me!"

"Well I don't want to choke her, but what if she slips from my grip? She'll kill me!"

"Just hold her tightly."

"But then we're back to me strangling her, and that's not a good idea, either."

Scott's filing technique convinced me we needed to swap roles. He was slow and methodical, while I impatiently needed him to finish the job immediately, before the process victimized either Graycie or me.

Once I commandeered the claw grinding job, I hit my stride. There's a lovely sense of control to be derived from manipulating her claws, as long as you trust that whoever is holding the vengeful parrot will not let go (and I could never quite assure Scott that I had a solid enough grip on her when I was doing that job). I'd spent years working in kids' grimy mouths as an orthodontic assistant for my dad, so I was used to wielding instruments in an awkward manner while dodging unexpected and unwanted obstacles.

My claw trimming duties meant I had to clasp and unfurl one curling claw at a time, while trying to keep her from digging the others into my flesh or squeezing them all together, thus rendering it impossible to get to the claw, also while gently placing the Dremel to the claw to grind it down as fast as possible. I had to be very careful to avoid the rapid rotary spinner sanding a burn on my fingers or the bird's feet, and often I had to unhook claws that had become entangled in the weave of the towel with which we were holding her. It was quite a managerial feat, especially in those early days.

Still, Scott hovered like an overprotective parent.

"Stop, before you draw blood."

"I'm not going to draw blood."

"See, now she's bleeding."

"I can't help it! I'm doing the best I can!"

For many years, in addition to claws, we also had to trim back Graycie's flight feathers. I used to think it seemed cruel to "clip" a bird's wings, but in fact this practice is merely like trimming fingernails. The intent behind wing clipping is to keep a parrot from flying inside a house, which is generally not particularly safe for it. Sure, plenty of parrot owners allow their birds to fly freely in their homes, but we didn't need to worry about being dive-bombed by the Dud on top of everything else.

To trim Graycie's flight feathers we had to again secure her with a towel, then draw the wing out and follow along the outer edge of the shorter "covert" feathers to see where to clip the longest ones, which are known as the flight feathers. We usually clipped from four to six feathers, leaving enough so that she'd have some loft in case she were to fall. Which would soon become quite a regular problem in our household, unfortunately.

Despite the fact that we did all this for her own good, Graycie wasn't particularly keen on our handling her. Perhaps part of this was because half the time our handling equaled dominating: holding her in a vise grip so that we could perform grooming techniques. No wonder she wasn't sharing the love.

Our ongoing attempts to warm her up to us just weren't showing much success. She was one smart bird. At times she reminded me of an irascible prisoner of war who may have had to accede to having been captured, but was having no part in drinking the Kool-Aid and becoming one with his captors. There would be no Stockholm syndrome with this parrot. In fact, if anybody was suffering from Stockholm syndrome, it was us. We had to remold our ways to hers, rather than vice versa. And somehow we were warming up to her coldness, even though it didn't do us a whole lot of good.

CHAPTER 5

Kitty Cocktails and Percolating Pups

In order to fully explain our commitment to Graycie, it helps to examine our history as pet owners. The truth is, Scott and I have a long and illustrious (and often hilarious) reputation of standing by our pets when lesser people would have packed up little birdie/kittie/doggie suitcases and sent them off to a nice farm in the country where they'd have plenty of friends to play with.

Always an animal lover, I wanted a cat since I was a small child. My father forbade all things feline in our dog-dominated household when I was growing up in Pittsburgh, so as soon as I graduated from Penn State and moved into an apartment in Northern Virginia, I brought home the first freebie kitten I could find, which I laid eyes on right outside the animal shelter. I'd gone to the shelter to get a kitten for my newly divorced mother for Christmas and hoped to get one for myself, but I didn't have enough cash for two. As luck would have it, as I was leaving the shelter, someone pulled into the parking lot with a whole litter. I asked the owner if she minded if I took one, and she obliged. I settled on the black kitten, as I'd always thought it'd be fun to have a black cat to follow under a ladder on Friday the thirteenth.

Life with my carefree kitten was good, until about a year later, when Mink went into heat—something to behold in a cat, if you've never experienced the magic of an estrogen-infused feline. She morphed from an unassuming little kitty into an outright bimbo, practically overnight. Mink would parade around the house, her tail hoisted high in the air, hitching her hindquarters up as if to announce her availability to anyone in her midst. I hadn't really thought about spaying her before because she was exclusively an indoor cat, but once the hormones kicked in, she became a dual-personality kitty, strutting around making loud, tormented moaning noises all day—and worse, all night. In those days I was always one signature away from bouncing my entire checkbook, so I was relieved when I learned about the government-subsidized spay program. I hauled Mink down to the county spay clinic, where, I thought, we would put an end to the all-night cater-wauling.

When the wailing persisted post-surgery, my roommates and I were extremely disappointed. Repeated phone calls to the vet were met with "it might take a while for the effects of the surgery to wear off." It didn't make sense to me that whatever was making the cat moan would fade away, rather than cease immediately upon removal of the offending organs. But in time, the noises persisted somewhat less frequently.

I had zero background in cat psychology; for all I knew Mink's issues weren't out of the ordinary. Scott had grown up with plenty of cats, and he'd seen all sorts of quirky feline behavior in his time so her issues didn't faze him too much, either. Besides, between my demanding job and spending what little free time I had with Scott, I could focus only so much time and energy on my cat's ongoing hormonal issues. Scott and I were spending many of our weekends road-tripping to the beach, visiting friends from college all over the East Coast, and sometimes taking trips to the countryside, which meant I was seldom home. This inevitably led to my roommates' conducting a little intervention one evening after work.

"Your cat acts like she's possessed by the devil," my roommate Twyla said. "She goes around making creepy noises all day and her eyes glint in an undeniably evil way. Something's gotta give."

"She's a sweet thing. She's just having some 'girl' problems," I said, not admitting that her green eyes did glint in a spooky way. But that's a black cat thing, isn't it? Part of their street cred?

"The cat's gotta go," the others insisted.

Finally I accepted that I wasn't going to win this argument, and Mink and I packed up our worldly possessions and joined my soon-to-be fiancé, Scott, and his roommates a few miles away at their spacious town house, along with Hobbes, a sweet calico kitten I'd given Scott for his birthday a few months earlier. Hobbes was trouble-free and entirely agreeable, one of those memorable gifts that lasts a lifetime (in a good way), and Scott and I totally adored her. In truth I'd felt guilty "harboring" a spare cat at Scott's place—like one of those duplicitous men who have a secret love child about whom his wife and kids don't know a thing—so it was good to finally get it out in the open; it was time for Mink to realize she was no longer an only cat.

The good news was, the cats got along fine (which for cats meant they basically ignored each other), and we hoped Mink would follow Hobbes's example and straighten up and be a bit more pleasant (and less creepy). But this was not in the cards. Instead she would only linger by the door, waiting to dart outside whenever someone came or went. And moan. Scott's roommates weren't particularly wild about the onslaught of felines, but since we spared them most of the housework, they humored us.

Then we went away for two weeks.

Scott had to escort two Sri Lankan entomologists who were researching malaria abatement through San Francisco and then to the rice paddies of U.C. Davis, and I went along for fun (presuming there was fun to be had with Sri Lankan entomologists). We left the cats behind, safe in the knowledge that they would be in good hands with his roommates. When we returned, both of his roommates were out. We called for the cats, and Hobbes came running, meowing and twisting figure eights around our ankles.

"Where's Minkie?" I asked, searching all over the house, to no avail.

Hungry after a long flight from California to D.C., Scott opened the refrigerator to find the fridge mostly bare but for a carton of milk on the top shelf. Taped to the side of the carton was an illustration of a black whiskered cat with a hobo stick perched atop her shoulders. Underneath, it read, *"Have you seen this cat? Dial 1–800-MISSING."*

Mink had finally succeeded in her escape plan, while Scott's roommate Dean was carrying luggage to the car to leave for a business trip himself. With no time to search for the cat, he'd instead sketched out his funny little milk carton missing-kitty poster, then left for the airport. Mink was long gone by the time we arrived back home. Luckily, Dean—one of Scott's best friends from childhood and his other business partner—is one of the funniest people we know. So even though our cat was among the missing possibly at any number of runaway way stations throughout America, eventually we couldn't help but laugh at the manner in which Dean delivered the news after we got over the initial shock of Mink's disappearance.

"I can't believe she finally did it," I moaned.

"We knew it was only a matter of time," Scott said as he wiped away my tears. He had a point. Mink had spent many of her waking hours trying to bolt out the front door. It wasn't exactly fair to expect a roommate who already didn't even like the cat to hold vigil to ensure the thing never crossed the threshold.

"But she's gone," I cried.

"Don't worry, she'll come back," Scott said, trying to cheer me up.

We searched everywhere for that crazy runaway. For months I pined for Minkie and would go outside in the evenings and call for her. But she never came.

One night, about a year later, Scott's other roommate, Buddy, and his girlfriend, Cindy, came home after being out to dinner and burst into the town house excitedly.

"Look who we found at the front door!" Cindy said.

In Cindy's arms was a bedraggled Mink, cobwebs and leaf bits tangled up in her whiskers, meowing nonstop, no doubt trying to explain away her absence.

We were relieved to finally have her home, and took her immediately to the vet—the same one who'd spayed her. I told him that she'd been wailing a lot and then ran away for a whole year. He said he'd "open her up and see what was wrong."

When Mink had surgery a few days later, we learned that the vet hadn't quite taken out all of her ovaries, so the poor thing had been half in heat all that time. I questioned how this could happen, despite my repeated entreaties about her moaning issues.

"What did you expect? You got the discount spay."

I was appalled, but the second time was the charm, and Mink stuck close to home for the rest of her twenty years of life and never moaned again.

~~~~~

Scott and I got married soon after Mink's return and officially merged our two cats into our family. Mink had settled down, finally, and Hobbes was the epitome of low-key. She even loved to fetch pieces of peppermint candy that were mailed to her once in a while courtesy of IBM—she'd somehow gotten on a mailing list as a secretary named Kitty Hobbes. We settled into a condominium with our indoor-bound cats and life was good. But then Hobbes started to make that old familiar yowling sound we knew so well from Mink as she became hormonally thrust into that mournful phase of cat-in-heat. Nature was taking over, demanding that her procreative needs be met.

One night over dinner, I came up with a marvelous idea to capitalize on Hobbes's unpleasant condition, and pitched my plan to my husband.

"So, uh, what do you think about maybe Hobbes's having kittens?"

I figured Scott would drop his knife on his plate or choke up a piece of steak upon hearing this nutty suggestion, but he didn't. Instead he laughed.

"You know, that would involve more than just Hobbes. And Mink's the wrong sex, in case you'd forgotten."

"I know that! But kitties would be so cute. We could keep them in the spare room. Think how much fun they'd be! And we could find homes for all the kittens. We know enough people who would want one."

Scott's family had kept several cats over the years, along with a litter or two of kittens, so he was well aware of the process. I could tell he was on the fence. Finally, he took a sip of water as he pondered our dilemma. "If you can figure out how to find her a nice boyfriend, I'm game. Deal?"

"Deal."

I set about seeking out a boyfriend for Hobbes, and despite a few dead ends, I eventually succeeded. During a period when the Senate was out of session and the senator I worked for had returned to his home state—one of those rare occasions when I could actually leave my desk to eat lunch—I went out for Chinese with my friend Susannah, and mentioned that I wanted my cat to have kittens.

"Wow, what great timing," she said. "I have a friend who has a friend in the State Department whose cat is going to be neutered next week. I bet he'd be happy to do the job."

Eureka! We'd found our donor. Sus put me in touch with Babs, who put me in touch with Patty, who assured us her randy cat, Oliver, would indeed enjoy one last walk on the wild side.

"I feel so badly that he'll never get it on again," Patty told me over the phone. "Oliver would be thrilled to work something out."

I know, a kitty hookup sounds foolish in hindsight. But back then it seemed like a brilliant idea.

A date was set: State Department Oliver was delivered to me in my Hart Senate Office Building cubicle (official Senate business), tied up in a pillowcase—neither of us could afford cat carriers on our meager government salaries—and prepared for an amorous liaison with the unsuspecting but totally hot for it Hobbes.

Now, we've all heard the expression about the cat's being out of the bag. But I'd never contemplated what it would be like to have a temperamental cat trapped *in* one. I learned quite rapidly, as I headed out into Friday rush hour, that cats don't like to be contained, especially in pillowcases. By the time I merged onto the Shirley Highway, I had an enraged, maniacal feline as a passenger, leaping and tumbling—still pillowcase-bound—and screeching like some modern-day fishwife. It was all I could do to maintain control of the steering wheel as the banshee in the backseat managed to tumble his way all over the place, dagger claws at the ready.

Upon my arrival home, after carrying him stiff-armed, like a sack of hazardous material, up three flights of stairs, I didn't know how to calm the mad cat down. I gingerly set Oliver onto the powder room floor, untied the string that was holding the bag shut, and dashed out the door.

Meanwhile, Hobbes's reaction to her weekend houseguest was less than enthusiastic. She'd been parading around our house for days, tail in the air, announcing to the world that she was looking for Mr. Goodbar, but when the real thing came knocking on her door, she turned tail and ran.

I, on the other hand, wasn't ready to give up so easily after all the effort I'd put into this rendezvous. But first Scott and I had to coax Hobbes down from her perch above the kitchen cabinet with a trail of fish-flavored Pounce. And once we did that, we realized that the only self-contained room in the house in which to conduct this strange affair was the powder room, where Oliver was already trapped.

I figured we needed to give Hobbes and Oliver a chance to become acquainted, to loosen up a little. But how? With kitty cocktails? I pictured the cats in happy hour mode, Oliver standing upright on hind legs, Hobbes perched on the edge of the bathroom vanity, one leg crossed elegantly over the other, the two engaged in witty repartee, tails twitching, toasting their cleverness, pausing for an occasional drag from a Gauloise.

Finally we shut the cats into the bathroom and hoped for the best. Every so often, Hobbes would emit peculiar hostile sounds, like maybe Oliver had stepped on her tail. But lacking a kitty cam, we weren't quite sure what was happening in there. And we certainly didn't want to spoil the mood by opening the door to investigate.

When we finally freed Hobbes from her little den of iniquity, she was entirely disheveled, complete with bits of kitty litter on her whiskers. She did not look happy. Alas, our little scheme had not played out according to plan. I felt deeply guilty for having put poor Hobbes through this needless trauma, and we returned Oliver to his owner, his last chance at romance evidently dashed by our very proper cat. No kittens resulted from this wayward attempt. Nor, apparently, did we learn a lesson in responsible pet ownership.

~~~~~

Next came Beau, our starter dog. Like many starry-eyed, clueless young couples, we figured a dog would be (a) such fun and (b) a great primer for parenthood. (Plus it seemed like the logical consolation pet, since we couldn't afford a parrot.) Like most of those couples, we'd soon learn that we were painfully naive about that whole dog-baby connection. I mean really, what is the link between a hirsute four-legged creature with undying devotion to its owner, a penchant for eating poop, and a regular—and bad—case of fleas, and a baby? Only the fact that both are high maintenance. So in that regard, I guess we were somewhat on the right track.

While Beau was cute and sweet and frisky, she soon proved to be one incredible challenge to both our olfactory systems and our checkbook. She had allergies, we would eventually learn, to basically everything in the world. For us to finally glean this would cost many thousands of dollars in vet bills over her ten-year life span, and crazy amounts of effort to keep her pollen-free, as the presence of grass, trees, mold, dust, mildew, and most all foodstuffs (including her own kibble) caused bad reactions.

At first her itching seemed to just be standard doglike scratching. Eager to enjoy the company of our new pet, we let her sleep in our bedroom at night. Until her itching caused her collar tags to jangle incessantly, and the noises from her gnawing on her itchy body would jar us awake at all hours. But we were the classic childless pet-obsessed dog "parents," so rather than get annoyed, we extended an olive branch of kindness.

"Oh, poor Beau-Beau," I'd croon after being awoken by the dog chewing on a hot spot so intensely she sounded like a percolating coffeepot. "What's the matter, baby?" And then I'd roll over and go back to sleep.

Boy, did things change when our son came along and we were smacked with severe sleep deprivation.

The *thump, thump, thump* of Beau's back leg against the hardwood floor as she attempted to satisfy that unquenchable itch in her ears at three in the morning quickly became unbearable.

"Stop it!" I'd holler at the dog.

"Aw, poor thing," Scott would say. *He* hadn't been up nursing the baby twice already, so his empathy meter was definitely more sensitive than mine.

"Scott, we have to get her out of here or I'll never sleep." Parenthood had instilled in me a covetous approach to sleep that's yet to diminish to this day.

So Beau ended up in the hallway, to guarantee us at least some modicum of sleep. Soon, however, her noisemaking was so pronounced—to the point where she woke Kyle *and* us— that Beau was relegated to the bottom floor of the house, right alongside the new parrot's cage.

Next came the ear infections. We went through countless tubes of greasy Panolog ointment trying to balance the chemistry in her ears so that she didn't smell toxic, but the correction would last only a few days before her ears turned an angry red and she'd shake her head so violently from the itch that she constantly had large, painful blood clots forming in her ear flaps.

She was also obsessed with paw gnawing, and the fur between her paw pads took on a deep scarlet tinge as a result of yet more infection. The dog was constantly infected from head to toe, all due to her autoimmune system's failing in its basic mission, thanks to inbreeding that was so common with Labrador retrievers back then. We yelled at her so often to stop scratching over the years that eventually even Graycie got in on the action, and she'd tell Beau to stop scratching several times a day.

We were periodically advised to consider putting Beau down because of her health problems. But she was our dog, and as such she was part of our family. We loved her, and we wanted to try to fix her problems.

So, before we'd even met Graycie we'd paid our dues to the animal kingdom in time, money, and emotional attachment. But all our pets have taught us much about ourselves as well. With each of our animals we've learned to love unequivocally, sometimes even when by all outward appearances it might have seemed as if what we were putting into the relationship was far more than we were getting out of it, when it seemed like it would be easier to walk away from the troubles than to endure the burden. But we also learned that it just wasn't in us to give up on something simply because it's become an inconvenience. Hassles come with the territory when it comes to domesticated animals, and obviously even more so with one from the wild. And yes, we would learn *that* the hard way.

CHAPTER 6

Name That Bird (or,
You Should Call Her *Thud*, not *Dud*)

Once Graycie became a reality in our lives, we had to figure out a proper moniker for her. The problem was, Scott and I were a bit name-weary by then. We'd just been through the whole name game during my pregnancy and had struggled mightily to reach a consensus.

"We should call him Tucker," I announced one day while we were sifting through baby name books once we knew we were expecting a boy.

Scott arched his eyebrow at me and shook his head no. "Yeah, I can hear the taunting on the playground already. Tucker the—"

"Fine. How about something Gaelic? I love Irish names. Like Seamus." I know. It's sort of odd to slap an ethnic name like that on a kid who bears little connection to the motherland. Although in my defense, I have a smattering of Irish branches in my family tree.

Scott didn't even deign to respond but instead just rolled his eyes.

"Matthew?" I suggested. "You can't go wrong with that name. It's one of the most popular names of the century!"

"Most popular means most *common*," Scott said, shaking his head again. "Besides, *Matt*? That's a sound, not a name."

After going through four books, disputing the finer details of the Latin derivations of the names, and dissecting each one ad nauseam, we narrowed it down to Kyle, Tyler, or Ryan. It just so happens that in 1989, those names weren't particularly popular, although shortly thereafter they became about as common as, well, Matthew.

~~~~~

So there we were, named out, and faced with the task of figuring out what to call our parrot. And the challenge was much more daunting than naming our previous pets, since we were told the creature could live for up to ninety years. (That's right. *Ninety years.*) We didn't want to give her a lame name and have her stuck with it for nearly a century.

Obviously Polly was out of the question. It was far too cheesy. Chaco was out, too, because the only Chaco we knew personally at the time was a frightening sociopath, and I didn't want to taint our parrot with any of that bad bird mojo. Besides, Chaco seemed a cliché name, as apparently every parrot in the history of pirating was named that.

It took about a month after Graycie's arrival for her name to finally come to us. As with everything else Graycie-related, this development involved pain.

Traditionally, house-kept parrots' wings are clipped to keep

them from flying indoors, and in theory this is a fine idea—
it's not cruel, as you're not damaging anything. After all, parrots' flight feathers grow much like human hair, and since we
couldn't turn her out into the wild, we had to make her environment as safe as possible. The only problem is that parrots
tend to flap their wings—probably to keep the muscles from
atrophying. And when our bird flapped her wings, she had the
troublesome habit of launching herself off the cage, only to fall
like a lead weight to the ground, since she had no loft.

Once Graycie started falling off the cage regularly, we realized our beautiful gray bird came across as rather clumsy, a
trait she shared with me. When I was growing up, I was a com-
petitive figure skater, and my mother often marveled at my
ability to execute a gravity-defying axel or an effortless sit spin,
only to walk off the ice and fall on my face—hence she nick-
named me Grace. So we found it fitting to give our new pet
the tongue-in-cheek name Graycie.

Alas, no longer a Dud in name, she was to remain one in
spirit for a while longer, never quite in fine feather. A glance at
Graycie's veterinary records from the five—yep, five—visits in
her first four months with us reveal the following:

"Feathers damaged: ten on wings and tail."

"Bird is somewhat agitated, continue to try to comfort."

"Has been looking ruffled."

And then, in early November, about ten months into her
life with us: "Self-mutilation, feathers all chewed down to
stubs. Blood feather broken at base, also feather cyst full of
blood. Lanced, pulled, silvadene, and wrapped wing in ban-
dages."

We didn't get it yet, but our bird hated being down in our
basement with a meager single window to the outdoors.

It was a perfectly fine room, and we spent much of our free time (which admittedly wasn't much, considering we had a newborn) in there with her. But it must have been awfully claustrophobic for a creature who was meant to fly free through vast outdoor expanses. It was there we would continue to try to hold Graycie, coercing her with goodies and kindness. And where she would merely growl, snap, and fall to the ground with regularity.

When Graycie came into our lives there wasn't much information available to us about raising African gray parrots—this was pre-Internet, and while you could find people who had birds, there wasn't a medium for sharing the kind of information we sought. Luckily we'd found one trusty book on parrot rearing, and we followed Dr. Stahl's sage advice when questions arose, but otherwise we were utterly clueless.

Our goal was to get Graycie onto our hands, but this is no small task with a bird who is naturally fearful of things with five potentially brutal fingers; the human hands with which she'd had previous experiences were indifferent at best, cruel at worst. So we had to build up her trust. We'd heard that parrots didn't care for gloved hands in particular—perhaps because those who worked in the trade of wild parrot smuggling routinely wore protective handgear—but without them, how could we get a fearful bird onto our hands safely?

The short answer is with patience and time. But the problem with that tack was that patience and time were in short supply around our home, what with a small baby perpetually wanting to nurse and seldom wanting to sleep. However, each day, when and if time became available, Scott and I would take turns gently yet nervously trying to encourage Graycie from her perch atop her cage onto an inch-thick, two-foot-long hardwood dowel. For a long time she merely growled at us and wouldn't budge off her cage. If we nudged her with the stick, she'd shriek and squawk, as if we were beating her. But African grays are bright and curious birds, and eventually she ventured onto the far end of the perch, where we'd have a standoff: her on one end, one of our hands on the other, as we quickly began experiencing muscle fatigue from the awkward position.

Grays tend to prefer one human to others, and back then Graycie seemed to choose me over Scott, at whom she'd sort of hiss and snarl. Of course I secretly relished her favoritism, but since I often had to be tending to Kyle because I was nursing him, I couldn't devote as much attention to her as Scott could. He would try to hold her, but it's not a pleasant experience to have to dodge a sharp beak, and it was far easier to just not bother with her. Besides, Scott was extremely busy with work, and spare time was not easy to come by. It was sort of benign neglect by default for Graycie. This is where parrothood and *parent*hood diverge: the parrot you can ignore. The baby, not so much. So when Kyle cried, we came running, leaving Graycie to fend for herself.

During those times when Scott would attempt to hold Grayce while I was tied up with the baby, he would get immensely frustrated with her lack of tolerance for him. With me, at least she'd be relatively silent, but with Scott, as soon as he got near her, she'd shriek. There's nothing that crushes someone's ego like someone—or something—freaking out whenever they're in your presence.

"If I upset her so much, what's the point in going near her?"

"I dunno. Maybe she'll get nicer?" All indications were that this prediction was unlikely to come true, but I figured I should encourage Scott nonetheless. "I'd try a little longer."

And to Scott's credit, he did tough it out with her, though it would take several years for Graycie to find Scott anywhere near as palatable as she found me, and I'm hardly her favorite creature.

Finally, after months of supporting the dead weight of a bird on the far end of a stick with one hand, she started inching her way toward the middle; the lure of a peanut helped. "Inching" might be an exaggeration—it was more like millimetering. Scott and I were ecstatic, our sense of hope in the bird renewed. After that modest milestone, there we would be, day in and day out during any free moment, one of us holding that stick, the trembling bird in the middle, dropping crushed peanut shells and pooping all over the floor. We were making great progress.

Our next goal was to persuade Graycie to let us touch her. The way Mark had explained it before returning to Africa after his holiday break, we had to cup our hands, with thumb and fingers tightly pressed together, and start stroking from her head along her back, finishing up with her red tail. This was something else that was a great theory. The reality of it worked somewhat differently. We would ever-so-gradually guide a cupped hand toward the bird, in full view of her so as not to startle her, and then squint our eyes as one would while playing Russian roulette, bracing for the worst (in this case the pain of the bite as we gingerly dragged our hands along her feathers).

Nature has imbued parrots with an incredibly quick reaction time. Thank goodness they're smaller than a liter bottle of water, which at least minimizes the amount of damage they can inflict. But regardless of her diminutive size, invariably Graycie would twist her head, randomly aim for whatever was in range, and snap, crocodile fast. Something about repeatedly exposing oneself to intentional injury triggers survival skills; you'd have to be sort of stupid to *want* to continue subjecting yourself to this. Yet we were so determined, and she was still so unhappy. For the most part she spent her days perched in or on the cage, looking scared, nervous, and bored, and we felt like real dogs for having culpability in her life's joy having been diminished in this way.

I sometimes wonder, had Mark not returned to Africa before Graycie's arrival, if Graycie would have experienced a bit of a boot camp indoctrination into life with the Gardiners. Mark is fearless and trusting when it comes to parrots, and doesn't tend to be intimidated by things like bodily harm from a wild bird, so he may have been able to pave the way for Scott and me to be able to interact with her in a friendly fashion. But Mark was far away and unable to serve as our surrogate parrot whisperer, so we were forced to muddle our way through ineffectually.

It didn't help matters when we'd visit Scott's nearby parents every few days and see that their bird was not only thriving, but had also settled in quite happily. At night Keith would hold the bird on his hand and gently pet its feathered head while watching television without so much as fearing a nip.

"I can't believe you can do that!" I moaned one evening. "Graycie won't let us get near her. And at those rare times that she does, she turns on us on a dime."

Scott's parents were totally empathetic, and if they could have done something to make Graycie straighten up and fly right, well, I'm sure they'd have done so. But the fact is, what

Graycie needed was our undivided and perpetual attention, and this was not going to happen any time soon. Perhaps if we had been empty-nesters, Graycie would have come around more readily. But all we could do was give her our catch-as-catch-can devotion and hope for the best.

CHAPTER 7

But Can She Pick Up Cable?

By the summer of her first year with us, we were beginning to have a little bit of luck. Occasionally, Graycie went willingly on the dowel. And sometimes she'd even let us attempt to pet her without inflicting severe bodily harm. Unfortunately for Graycie, our son was becoming increasingly mobile, so the available time we had to handle a feisty bird shrunk exponentially with Kyle's ability to first crawl, then walk. He was always one step away from trouble, especially considering he was also always one step away from a bird that could do major damage to a toddler. So what progress we had made began to deteriorate as a result of unplanned-for neglect.

In July I learned I was pregnant again. This meant a larger house was in order. Scott and I were thrilled about the upcoming arrival of our second child, and excited to find the perfect place to welcome our new addition home. However, the incumbent house hunting meant yet more demands on our time that precluded lots of interaction with Graycie. Plus the sheer exhaustion from my first trimester had me desperate to sleep whenever my son napped, which was about the only free time I'd previously had for the parrot.

We wanted a contemporary house (we weren't fans of the traditional, low-ceilinged homes that were the hallmark of Northern Virginia) with four bedrooms, plus a home office for Scott. And after enjoying Buddy and his wife Sheila's swimming pool over the summer, I began to harbor a backyard pool fantasy as well, though I was doubtful we'd find a home that fulfilled our entire wish list. So when we set foot into a contemporary home with lots of windows, four bedrooms, a fabulously updated kitchen, and—ta da!—a swimming pool, I was elated.

"This is perfect! It has everything we want!" I crowed to Scott and the lady of the house as we stood at the sleek black-tiled kitchen counter and I eyed the brushed chrome cooktop, devising all sorts of plans for it.

Scott kicked me hard in the shin and gave me the stink-eye. Apparently I'd killed any chance of negotiating a good deal on the price. But what could I say? It felt like kismet.

Plus, the people who owned the house had parrots. Clearly it was meant to be.

~~~~~

With our living situation under control, I felt slightly better. However, as luck would have it, Graycie's first major medical trauma happened just before we made the move to the Fairfax home. She'd chewed her wing feathers down to nubs, necessitating a stressful wing-bandaging.

There's never a good time for a pet to have a medical issue, but this was particularly bad timing. I was five months pregnant and had a fifteen-month-old under my supervision by day while Scott worked, and I was trying to pack a house to move in a matter of weeks, all the while going to the new house to paint and wallpaper the kids' rooms and strategize the eradication of a flea infestation left in the absence of the previous owners' two dogs. Administering daily oral antibiotics to a feisty, bleeding, and uncooperative bird was the last thing I needed to add to my plate.

Soon our vet determined that Graycie's ongoing feather plucking meant that a protective collar was in order. Because the move to the new house would probably further stress out our already stressed-out bird, we decided to leave her with Dr. Stahl during the week we moved into our new digs. At that time he placed a custom-made Elizabethan collar—one of those radar dish contraptions—on poor Graycie, the theory being that the collar would keep her from being able to access her wings and thus cease the feather mutilation. I was hoping it would at least help us to get basic cable channels, but no such luck. I thought it was fitting it was called an Elizabethan collar, as our bird's bite and ferocity of spirit were comparable to the notorious eponymous queen's.

While we moved and unpacked and prepared our new home for ourselves, the bird, and the holidays, Graycie completely clammed up at the vet's, despondent over this latest setback in her life. Within a week, she had figured out how to get around her expensive custom collar and chew feathers to her heart's content, so right after she got home, we had to send her back for the standard version, which was cheaper and bigger. We'd been hoping not to have to make her even more miserable, but what could we do? She was bleeding profusely on a regular basis.

When she returned from her latest vet appointment Graycie was miserable over the collar she was forced to wear, but we soon discovered that her new abode—in a prime spot overflowing with natural light—was just what the doctor ordered. With high ceilings and windows and skylights galore, the new house was as close as Graycie could get to the great outdoors without actually being there. Soaring space seemed to equal soaring spirits. And it was only going to get better for her—the previous residents, who had two cockatoos, had built a very large outdoor parrot cage in the backyard, which we hoped to make great use of when the weather got warmer.

Graycie absolutely loved her new location, which was smack in the center of the action, with the kitchen, dining room, and living room all within her sight line. And along with her happiness came her words. Up until then she'd yell out my name (in Scott's voice) occasionally, but she wasn't particularly conversant. Now that she lived near both the back door and the dining room table, Graycie picked up snippets of conversations relevant to those locations and repeated them, to hilarious effect.

"Beau! Waitwaitwaitwaitwait!" I probably yelled at my dog several times a day during inclement weather, as the dog regularly tried to rush past me into the house to avoid having her muddy paws wiped clean. I never realized I said it so frequently until Graycie repeated the line in my voice for the first time, and then continued to do so every time I opened the door to let the dog in, leaving us doubled over in laughter. She was near the microwave as well, and each time we approached it, she'd start making the beeping sounds of the various buttons we pushed to make it start before we even had a chance to.

And then came the telephone.

One day while I was fixing dinner the phone rang. As I reached for it, just before I picked it up from the cradle, I heard Scott's voice say, "Hello? Hi! How are ya! Uh huh, uh huh, uh huh. Okay, bye bye." It was the parrot.

I couldn't believe the bird memorized his phone conversations. Then I realized this could come in handy . . . a spy parrot might be kind of fun.

Without our fully realizing it as it was happening, Graycie's growing repertoire captured this time of our lives in a snapshotlike way, and we fell into comfortable habits with her. When I would walk over toward the microwave, I would often say, "Hey, Gray! How are ya?" Soon, whenever I took a step in the direction of the microwave, she'd beat me to it and say hello to herself in my voice. Graycie was soon whistling for Mink to come in from outside (by then we let the cat out into our fenced-in backyard, figuring it would satisfy her wanderlust while keeping her safe from predators), and asking Kyle in my voice, "Whatssamatter?" whenever he cried. She was capturing our daily life in an audible time capsule. Finally Graycie was becoming a participating member of the family, too.

One evening during our first year in the new house I was cooking dinner with National Public Radio's *All Things Considered* on in the background. A segment of the program featured the winner of a national whistling contest, and the minute the winner began to whistle, Graycie became instantly alert. Within thirty seconds, she was whistling along note for note, a beautiful response to the music being broadcast by the radio. I was transfixed watching Graycie momentarily transported by what she heard, and surprised at her whistling talents, which had lain dormant until then.

When I heard that first evocative trill emitting from our

small gray-feathered creature, I thought, *This could be the start of a great relationship.* Over the years I've revised this sentiment to something along the lines of *Hmm, if she doesn't bite my jugular, shit on my head, or maim my children, I guess we'll keep her, if for no other reason than out of guilt.* But it was a start, and as I said, we were making progress.

Or so I thought.

CHAPTER 8

Awww, Crap

One of those dirty little secrets about parrots that you don't realize is that they're, well, dirty. Maybe in the wild their mess is dispersed over such a wide area that it's seldom apparent, but in the confines of your average home, the reality of a parrot's daily functions is a bit unwelcome. Keeping a parrot in the house means you're in for a lot of cleaning, unless you want to live in one of those places where social services ends up being called in to haul out first a disheveled, greasy-haired, haggard-looking you, followed by your two hundred cats, fifteen mangy dogs, and thirty-five filthy cages filled with emaciated birds of all types. One of those houses that even rodents find too dirty to occupy.

Having a parrot means being prepared to clean up excrement several times an hour. This is not an exaggeration. Parrots probably poop three times an hour. That's practically seventy-five poops a day. If we lined up each of Graycie's excretions over the past two decades end to end, it would circle the globe three times. Actually, I made that up, but it often feels like that statistic is about right.

If only I could keep in my employ someone whose task it is simply to catch bird doo before it makes a huge mess everywhere, life would be so much easier. I wish I could've done this particularly when my children were small and drawn to the very things you want them nowhere near. It's not like we could have put Mr. Yuk stickers all over the cage and hoped for the best. Time and again Kyle would make his way right over to the parrot cage, where at any given moment there would be excrement (old or new), discarded fruits and veggies, parrot chow, and stray fallen feathers within reach. Heaven forbid we fed her blueberries (a favorite), as then we'd have to be especially vigilant about catching that poop before it stained the hardwood floors, all the while monitoring our toddler's whereabouts.

Cage sanitation is often an exercise in humiliation. Had I known I would be spending two decades in perpetual pursuit of a poop-free home, ol' Graycie might just have remained but a glimmer in our eyes (or an unclaimed parrot in quarantine). I actually know someone who successfully trained her African gray to use the toilet, yet this woman still eventually got rid of the bird.

I've often joked that if Graycie were a human teenager, the door to her room would have to be kept shut. I don't doubt her underwear would be dangling from a light switch and piles of papers and food wrappers would be strewn about the floor along with discarded tissues, hair elastics, a banged-up iPod with missing headphones, and other detritus of teendom. As it is, she has always been prominently on display in the main thoroughfare of our home. This means she's visible from many places in the house.

In addition to the food messes she creates, the bird shreds cage-lining newspapers with such vehement regularity I think I could sub her out to a few Beltway Bandits in D.C. for disposal of classified documents. On top of that, the dander that falls off her leaves a coating of feather dust surrounding her cage like the winter's first light dusting of snow, and usually gets stirred up in the air, spreading into the rest of the main floor as well. When she eats, she tosses off much of what she is consuming, which means bits and pieces of food on the walls, on the floor, sometimes on the furniture. And if she tosses away bits of a fiery habanero pepper, heaven help the poor slob who picks that up off the ground (usually me), because that hot pepper oil stings something fierce if you then rub your eyes. I keep telling Graycie to not waste her food—there are starving parrots in Africa—but she tunes me out.

Cool new tricks notwithstanding, the last thing I needed while I set up our new home and prepared for the birth of my second child was a bird who needed a personal valet. Hell, *I* needed a valet.

~~~~~

Our daughter Kendall was born in March, five months after we moved into our new home, in a perfectly civil and easy delivery. This contrasted radically with Kyle's delivery, to my great relief, as his laborious entry into the world approximated birthing elephant twins, and I was not up for a repeat performance of that. The only downside to my pregnancy with Kendall was a case of gestational diabetes, which meant I was sworn off sugar for many months. The minute she was born, my father-in-law kindly showed up with an entire quart of

Baskin-Robbins rocky road ice cream, just for me. How much better could life get?

We were settling in happily, but there was still the problem of the fleas our previous owners left as a little housewarming gift for us. I'd first discovered them about a month before we moved when I'd gone over for the day to wallpaper and had brought Beau along, thinking she'd be lonely at home. I got caught up in what I was doing, and after a few hours I went in search of the dog, who had gone to sleep on the carpet in one of the bedrooms. When she stood up, she was coated with hundreds upon hundreds of undulating black dots, and her blonde coat was looking darker by the minute.

I'm one of those bug-averse types who can't even touch the pages of *National Geographic* when they feature magnified images of insects and bacteria. So when I first saw this moving coat of insects clinging to my dog, I couldn't even identify what they were (no doubt a classic case of denial), and simply screamed. Next I called my husband.

"Oh, my god. You should see this dog. There are small black *things* all over her!"

"Small black whats?"

"Like creepy, crawly icky things that are moving all over her en masse."

"Like fleas?"

I have no idea why it hadn't dawned one me that she was coated in fleas. Beau came as a puppy just full of them, and between Hobbes and Mink, we'd had enough fleas in carpets to ensure bites on everyone's ankles for months on end. Unluckily for us, those fleas had been left dogless just long enough to multiply yet not die. We sprung into action and that same day had the vets dip the dog and the cats, had the carpets thoroughly cleaned, and hoped the fleas would die off before we moved in.

But by late summer the fleas were on a very successful slash and burn campaign. Summertime just invited more of them to join the party, as every time Beau went outside, in came distant relatives of those rat bastard fleas that had already colonized the place. We were under siege, with the occupying force consisting of these damned little insects that refused to die and constantly planted their occupying flags on the dog and cats. Yet with two small children, one of whom was still nursing, and a highly sensitive parrot (the birds are always the first to go), the last thing we wanted to do was assault the place with those famously toxic flea bombs that then permeate every square inch of your home, including all dishes and eating surfaces, with unhealthy chemicals. But we had to do something or soon the fleas would claim ownership of the house.

These ongoing hassles became overwhelming, on top of the usual demands of small children, pets, and Scott's growing business, which was requiring him to travel more often. At times tensions were tight between us, as we became increasingly frustrated at our inability to control our out-of-control circumstances.

"Can't you figure out something to make this better?" I implored, as if it was his job to figure out the solution to our flea problem.

"Don't blame me! I can't help it they're everywhere."

Of course not, but surely someone needed to take responsibility. At least in the illogical mind of a tired, overworked mom. Thankfully my nagging paid off, and Scott, ever the resourceful one, eventually stumbled upon what was supposed to be a holistic alternative flea treatment involving boric acid powder.

Back when I landed my job on Capitol Hill right out of college and moved to Washington, I lived in a few places with serious cockroach problems. I was used to turning on a light only to see those vile insects scurry for the nearest cabinet in which to hide. And I learned early on that lining the base of the apartment walls with boric acid powder—which was supposedly nontoxic, so my cat wouldn't die if she came in contact with it—would make the cockroaches shrivel up and die in a snap. Sure enough, it worked.

The treatment that Scott discovered entailed workmen coming into the house with some special machinery that would grind large volumes of boric acid powder into all carpeted surfaces of the home, which would result in a totally dehydrated (and very dead) network of fleas who would no longer bother us or the dog. Even though this would require our vacating the premises, it sounded promising to us (we were desperate, after all). Our strategy was thus: Scott was to go on a previously scheduled business trip, with me to follow a few days later for a fleeting and much-needed long-weekend getaway to Arizona.

Before I left, I packed for my trip, hauled the parrot and cats off to the vets, and got the kids and the dog packed and sent off to my in-laws' house. Oh, and I covered every surface in the entire house to keep it all from being coated in a fine dust of boric acid, which would then require having to take on a massive cleanup task upon my return from that relaxing vacation getaway I was so badly in need of. Check.

I used plastic sheeting to top all the beds and taped off areas that indicated no flea-infested zones (our main floor was hardwood so it was exempt), and I was still scrambling to block off dust-free zones as the workmen arrived in their Hazmat gear and masks to start their massive eradication measures, using machines that resembled large lawn mowers. As I peered down the hall at the thick cloud of boric acid dust whipping around like dirt from an Oklahoma dustbowl storm, I had the uneasy feeling that I was gonna have a lot of cleanup awaiting me after my little carefree vacation.

And boy was I ready for a vacation. Like most moms with small children, I felt so overly needed, all I wanted was a few days to be *not* needed. I felt like everybody—the kids, the pets, even Scott—constantly wanted a piece of me, and by the time I'd finished packing I had no more pieces to give. It's exhausting to be wanted so badly. In an ideal world, mandatory vacation time would be the god-given right of all mothers. So yeah, as much as I loved my children, I was beyond ready for a need-free weekend away.

Scott and I had a marvelous time in Arizona. For three straight days I sat on a ledge in a warm pool at the resort and read, and worked on a quilt I was making for Kyle, and enjoyed the cold drinks the cabana boys brought me. We rented a jeep and ventured into Red Rock Country in Sedona, had leisurely meals during which no babies cried and no parrots demanded attention and no dogs barked and nobody bled, and wow, it was great. We were responsibility-free after two pretty intense years of lots of have-to's. Like many couples with small children, we had mostly forgotten what it was like to spend time with each other in which the core topic didn't revolve around diapers, croup, or Barney, and it was nice to realize that we could still have fun like grown-ups. At least once every couple of years or so.

But as they say, no good rest goes unpunished.

We landed in Virginia relaxed and were thrilled to reclaim our children from Scott's parents' house, and even looking forward to gathering our brood of beasts from their various repositories. Everyone collected and accounted for, we happily headed toward home.

We arrived at a house that looked like an outtake from *Scarface*—worse yet, it looked like some south-of-the-border cocaine manufacturing plant that had exploded. White dust coated every surface in our house. Everything. Sure, the stuff was supposedly nontoxic, but it was in every nook and cranny and on every single surface. It had crept into the cabinets and covered our dishes and food. Scott and I glanced at our toddler, baby, and vulnerable parrot and knew our work was cut out for us. Before we could even go to bed we had to wash all the bedding, all the dishes, and all the countertops, mop the floor, and generally wipe out all benefits of that fabulous little vacation we'd just enjoyed.

And while the unbelievable amount of cleanup we faced was an unwelcome challenge, the fact that small children and pets exact their own little behavioral revenge when parents/owners disappear for vacations was in many ways worse. After being left behind, kids and animals tend to want to reassert their dominance over their parents/keepers upon their return, and do so with tantrums, misbehavior, and general mayhem. It's a good thing I relished that massage I'd had in Arizona, because I needed to channel that Zen moment for the next month.

CHAPTER 9

The Bird Has More Lives than Your Average Cat

A day and a half after we returned to our powder-filled but flea-free home, Kyle got sick. We'd been pretty lucky up to that point; he hadn't had any major ailments, just a few colds here and there. However, I'd been a mother long enough to realize that whatever he had wasn't your run-of-the-mill stomach bug. But mothers are preconditioned to not be too alarmist with pediatricians lest the doctors roll their eyes and walk away while shaking their heads, so despite the fact that I had to change Kyle's diapers at least fifteen times the day after our return home, I didn't call the doctors. Exhausted from ridding our home of the blanket of white powder the night before, Scott and I just hoped that whatever it was would go away after a day or so.

Unfortunately, the only thing that changed overnight was the rate at which we were changing diapers. In fact, Kyle's medical chart from the time states that I was changing diapers three to five times an hour. The poor thing was pooping as frequently as the bird, who, incidentally, was being entirely neglected, after having been boarded at the vet and then coming home to the great flea powder debacle. And now this.

On day two I took Kyle to the pediatrician, an elderly gentleman who probably attended med school when leeches were commonly used and no doubt felt he'd already seen it all. The doctor, intent on doing the standard top-down once-over on his patient, began with my son's ears. He couldn't see in because they were clogged, so he pulled out a long sharp instrument with which he planned to probe further.

"Um, I don't think you should bother with that," I said, wary that my child was panicking at what was to come. "His ears aren't the problem." Trust me, I knew everything wrong was down on the opposite end.

But the doctor insisted, and as I suspected, Kyle freaked out from the pain inflicted by that metal instrument and hid under the chair, refusing to come out.

"He just has a little bug," the doctor finally said as he washed his hands, using that classic tone of condescension most mothers have heard from at least one pediatrician over the years.

"Well, I'm hardly an expert, but my gut tells me this isn't just a little bug," I insisted.

"If things persist, we can consider doing a stool sample in a couple of days."

Frustrated, I changed yet another diaper and carted my son and my baby daughter back home, my mothers' instinct telling me things were worse than we knew. By night things had gotten worse, and we called the pediatrician's office, insisting that we get a stool culture. Reluctantly, they agreed.

For the next few days we did our best to keep Kyle hydrated. I could barely get one diaper on him when I'd have to change yet another. There was nothing in him, yet still he was buckled over in pain and expelling whatever was left in his system. And if I wasn't changing one of Kyle's diapers, I was changing Kendall's, or wiping up bird poop off the floor around the cage. (Thankfully, scooping cat litter was primarily Scott's job because I'd been pregnant or nursing so much over the previous few years and cat poo isn't good for moms.) We somehow muddled through what were definitely some of the longest days of our lives, and then early Sunday morning, the phone rang.

"Mrs. Gardiner?" the doctor said when I answered. It's not often that doctors call patients on Sunday morning, so I was all ears.

"I'm afraid your son has salmonella poisoning," he said. "This is highly contagious and by law we have to put you in touch with the health department, who will need to know where your son has been and how he might have contracted it."

Scott and I had been luxuriating in spas and swimming pools with the cabana boys in Arizona, so we certainly didn't know. Some parents we were.

The doctor told us the health department would track our family until Kyle was determined to be salmonella-free, which could take weeks, maybe even months. He said that in such a young child, the use of antibiotics was contraindicated, and chances were he was getting over the worst of the infection at that point. He also said we had to use precautions when handling his dirty diapers because of the contagion factor. Were he in day care or preschool, he'd have been banned until better. Luckily, we didn't have to deal with that kind of humiliation.

We never did determine how he contracted the salmonella, though the best guess was from a petting zoo he'd gone to with his grandparents while we were on vacation. Figures, with us, there simply had to be some sort of animal culpability.

~~~~~

Once Kyle started to rebound, we were able to breathe a sigh of relief. But as luck would have it, Kendall started having strange digestive problems a few weeks later. She'd gone from nursing to eating baby food with no problems, and we'd been supplementing with baby formula without issue. But now Kendall began to throw up almost everything she ingested. And what did get through her did so angrily, so much so that she was getting second-degree burns instead of simple diaper rash because of the acid rushing through her digestive tract.

This was compounded, unbeknownst to us, when the doctor put her on a highly digested version of baby formula, which we might as well have poured into crystal champagne flutes and toasted each other with—the stuff was the Dom Pérignon of baby formulas, and the price reflected it. By this point I was feeling rather desperate to (a) have potty-trained children and (b) never have to clean up poop, be it human, dog, cat, or parrot, ever again.

After several weeks of juggling foods and formula, we were able to get Kendall's problem under control. Just in time for Graycie to let us know she was tired of having been forgotten in the chaos that our lives had become.

We'd continued to trim Graycie's flight feathers as we had been doing since she'd joined our family. But now the parrot cage was surrounded by hardwood floors, and just to add insult to injury, a hard brick wall. So while in our old home Graycie occasionally fell off her cage onto soft carpet, at the new house she'd fall onto a solid wood surface, frequently bouncing off the brick wall on her way down. She would start to flap her wings and take off, only to plummet like a watermelon plunging from a window. The force of one particularly nasty fall onto a hard surface introduced a new problem into our lives: her breastbone punctured her flesh, leaving a large, gaping wound. If we thought we had problems with feather plucking, we hadn't seen anything yet.

This happened just before Thanksgiving, when we were still in the midst of Kendall's diaper crisis. The fall occurred in the morning as I was feeding Kyle breakfast while trying to keep Kendall contained in a high chair. As usual, I'd opened up Graycie's cage on top, so that she could walk out onto the perch. One minute she was imitating Scott's loud belch, to our great amusement, and the next thing we knew, she began flapping her wings furiously—something that always got the kids giggling—and then *whomp!*, she toppled off the cage and landed. Hard. Which of course caused the dog to come running, the kids to start crying, and general commotion to ratchet up to unpleasant levels so early in the day.

I reached with a wooden dowel to transfer Graycie back from the floor to the cage, and as she grabbed on with one foot, I noticed a trail of blood beneath her.

"Scott!" I yelled. "Get up here, fast!"

Graycie was bleeding pretty significantly and was understandably distraught, which meant blood was getting everywhere. Meanwhile, the kids were wailing, the dog was barking, and it was complete mayhem.

Scott raced upstairs and grabbed a towel, and we wrapped

Graycie up sufficiently to protect us from her beak and to get a better look at the wound, which even to our uneducated eyes didn't look good. We had no idea if she had a superficial wound or if it went much farther. Aware that birds are terribly susceptible to infections, we knew we had to get her to the vet's immediately, so we packed up the kids, leaving breakfast behind, and raced out of the driveway, hoping we could patch up our poor bird. After being so busy worrying about Kyle and then Kendall and all of the other make-work hassles in our lives, suddenly we wondered whether our little parrot friend would last the day.

"Maybe you should drive a little faster in case she's near death," I said to Scott.

"She's not going to die," he assured me. "And I somehow don't think the cops are going to buy the parrot emergency plea when they issue me a speeding ticket."

"But look at her, she's bleeding a lot."

"She's a tough bird. She'll come out of this fine."

I don't know if either of us truly believed that.

The news was not good at the vet's: Graycie had a very deep open wound at the bottom of her sternum. Her chart read, "Will need aggressive therapy."

As if we hadn't been dealing with enough aggressive therapy with our human charges of late, now we had another patient to tend to. One who couldn't express how she felt in any way other than trying to bite us.

Dr. Stahl was wonderful with Graycie. He and his assistants cleaned up her injury, sutured the wound, and sent us home with very specific care instructions. He was hopeful that she'd be all right, but there were no assurances.

And so began the next odyssey in the care and maintenance of our gray bird. Two weeks of oral antibiotics, twice daily. Antibiotic drops on the wound, twice daily as well. And then the clincher: hydrotherapy three times a day, morning, noon, and night, for as many weeks. To perform this therapy, we had to capture our unwilling patient with a clean towel, being careful not to upset her and cause her to fall off the cage yet again, and also not to make contact with the open wound, thus risking infection. We'd then set the towel aside, so as to not saturate it, and try to hold a slippery-feathered bird with a firm enough grip to not let her loose but not so tightly that we'd hurt her. Then one of us would hold Graycie over the sink in the usual headlock position to keep her from biting, while the other would spray warm water directly onto the puncture, trying to flush it clean and prevent infection from setting in. Of course this hurt the poor parrot, who let it be known she was not happy with us by attempting to squirm out of our grip and squawking wildly in distress. It was not a pleasant experience for any of us. And generally while we were tending to Graycie, we were unable to tend to our children, who couldn't exactly be pinned down in a safe zone while we were preoccupied with the bird. I used to joke that I needed a Velcro wall to hold them down during such occasions.

We boarded Graycie at the vet's over Thanksgiving when we went out of town. When we picked her up, her chart said she was crabby. This was not surprising, but when we saw that they'd even put a frowny face next to her information, we knew Graycie had *not* been a happy camper. Usually Graycie at least enjoyed their loving attention, but clearly this had not been the case.

By Christmas our rehabilitation efforts had proven effective and her wound was mostly healed. She got a clean bill of health from Dr. Stahl, who suggested we not trim her claws, as he presumed without them being sharp enough, she was unable to get a good enough purchase while standing on her cage and that's why she was falling off. Not having to subdue Graycie to perform that burdensome task was fine by me.

After we felt certain that Graycie had healed, we opened her cage up again. She'd been pretty despondent being stuck in there all day except for her hydrotherapy sessions, and she brightened up with the relative freedom this allowed her. But her freedom was short-lived. In February, only two months after she was declared fit, Graycie took another bad spill. Once again, we rushed her to Dr. Stahl, who flushed her wound, stitched her up, and this time boarded Grayce for five days to monitor her. With this being a repeat injury, Dr. Stahl was even more concerned about her healing properly. Once she returned home, we were again tasked with the hydrotherapy/antibiotic routine, only now we had *two* small children running loose, since by then Kendall was walking. We felt awful about Graycie's ongoing injuries but were equally stressed out trying to tend to her and ride herd over our kids. Our children were generally pretty cooperative, but they were indeed children, who don't think through cause and effect, so the possibility of injury wasn't exactly on their minds. While we tended to the parrot's medical maintenance, Kyle and Kendall would run loops around the main floor of our house until they got dizzy and fell down or until they crashed into each other, either of which inevitably led to tears. Scott and I were not amused.

Amazingly, Graycie healed again. But we still weren't trimming her claws, so she became impossible to hold. I'd try to get her on my hand, which by then she'd occasionally agree to do, and she'd scurry up my arm, piercing holes in my flesh as she went. It's surprising people didn't suspect I was a heroin junkie, with all of those puncture wounds. Once she'd made her way up my arm, Graycie would perch atop my back, right by my neck, my vulnerable jugular vein within striking distance of her wayward beak, all the while snagging my clothes, pooping down my back, and causing me to wince in pain with her shifting her weight and those lethal claws.

Yep, we were bonding in a big way.

~~~~~

When Mark brought us all parrots for Christmas, Scott's parents' parrot, Ballou, was the one with the most promise, and ours was the fixer-upper parrot (his sister's parrot, which arrived many months after ours, ended up falling somewhere in the middle). Right around the time of Graycie's fall, gorgeous, smart, friendly Ballou suffered a very premature death. He'd begun to lose feathers, which, judging from our parrot, wasn't in and of itself a sign of anything fatal, necessarily. But parrots often hide illness, a trait that is part of their natural defenses for life in the wild, and so a bird can be in decline for a good while before one realizes there's a problem. Ballou had been losing weight, and was finally diagnosed with the highly contagious and usually fatal beak and feather disease, a sort of birdie AIDS. It was a long decline for Ballou, who soon lost all his feathers, rendered completely bald.

Ballou passed away while Mia and Keith were on vacation; the poor petsitter found the bird at the bottom of the cage. It was a sad loss for Scott's parents. Scott and I were saddened as well, and Ballou's loss reinforced our determination to help Graycie heal and to take good care of her. Sure, she wasn't the docile, friendly type that Ballou was, but we realized how sad we'd be if she died, and were reminded not to take anything for granted.

~~~~~

The summer following Ballou's death was relatively easy. Both kids were becoming somewhat self-sufficient, and we had that wonderful pool right in our backyard, which was a mixed blessing because we had to be constantly vigilant about our children's whereabouts, but it was a lovely place to spend a hot afternoon. And we frequently invited friends and family over. I found out I was expecting baby number three, and when the kids had their afternoon naps I'd go outside and rest on a pool float. Maybe I should've been using that time to work on be-friending Graycie, but I was caring for myself a bit, because the pregnancy was taking a lot out of me and the exhaustion was sometimes overwhelming.

One day I was out doing errands and came home to blood splattered all over the white walls, the dining room table, the hardwood floors, the dining room chairs, and the large dec-orative antique quilt we'd mounted on the wall. Diagnosis? Cracked blood feather.

It seemed that one way or another Graycie was going to elicit attention from us. If only we could have managed her in a positive way, rather than just reacting again and again to her self-inflicted injuries, I suppose everyone would've been bet-ter off. But as anyone who has small children or has ever been pregnant or has been responsible for a house, a dog, and a husband knows, sometimes reacting is the best you can do.

~~~~~

A few months later, Christmastime was once again upon us. We always whipped ourselves into a frenzy over the holidays, with lots of decorating and gift purchasing and craft projects and entertaining and general forced frivolity. Kyle was in preschool, so we also had Christmas pageants and costumes and banquets for which to plan. Not to mention Santa visits, relatives to attend to, and toys to assemble.

Oh, and a birdcage to wash.

This is a chore that under the most pleasant conditions (seventy-five degrees and sunny, bluebirds overhead, daffodils in bloom) is not one that I embrace. In frigid weather, water doesn't come out of a hose unless one bangs it against the driveway to dislodge embedded ice. Mr. Clean soapsuds tend to cling in bubbly icicles, suspended mockingly from the brass rungs of the cage. Hardened bird excrement, which is supposed to wash away with the hose (and a *lot* of elbow grease), tends to freeze in little poopsicles on top of its already solidified state. It's not pretty. And yet I found myself that holiday season repeatedly performing this task, well into my pregnancy, my back aching, water barely trickling from the hose yet managing somehow to splash on my face and leaving behind cruel little icicles on my eyelashes. Happy holidays indeed.

In the midst of all of our holiday cheer, Graycie wanted to get in on the action, too. Just as quickly as you could say *"flap, flap, flap, thud,"* we were back at the vet. Her chart from her holiday visit reads, "Busted keel bone again, at very distal part.

Deep." Dr. Stahl debrided the wound, stitched it up, and sent her back to us, this time with explicit orders to keep Graycie in the cage indefinitely.

Two weeks later, she fell off her perch, inside her cage.

And then, just in time for a completely relaxing holiday season, Kyle came down with chicken pox.

CHAPTER 10

Gray Days

Our friends all assured us it was best to have both kids sick with chicken pox at the same time. Since we were all in favor of simplifying our lives wherever possible, Scott and I entertained the idea. So we bathed the kids together, made sure they drank out of the same cup every now and then, and did whatever we could to give Kendall Kyle's case of chicken pox, smugly scheduling our child's disease into the calendar. Sure enough, by mid-January Kendall was covered in red spots.

We quickly learned that maybe it wasn't such a clever idea to saturate Kendall in germs, because within days she was hospitalized from vomiting so much she was nearly dehydrated. It's a good thing Graycie was confined to her cage, because we had no time to deal with hydrotherapy—we had to worry about hydrating our little girl.

We weathered this latest health crisis, but just as Kendall's sickness was becoming a memory, Graycie, as her medical chart describes it, "took another nosedive." Dr. Stahl decided that the claw trimming wasn't at the root of the problem, but rather the wing trimming, and he advised us to stop trimming Graycie's flight feathers. This time, the proscription was the solution to the problem. Although to this day, when preening, Graycie chews the feathers down on her left wing, so that if she were to attempt to fly she'd probably circle in one direction like a canoe being paddled by one oar.

In retrospect I wonder if we were really dense not to have figured out on our own how to stop Graycie from dropping from her cage, or maybe we were simply slow learners. Most likely at the time we were caught up in so many things occurring in our lives that we must have just missed obvious signs, or not had a moment to consider the problem. Because shortly before Graycie's last dive-bomb, it was my turn for a medical emergency.

Labor pains are a funny thing; even after having a couple of babies, it's not always easy to be certain that what one is feeling is actually a baby wanting to be born. Late one evening, Scott was just getting into bed when I leaned over to break the news to him.

"I hate to say it, but you'd better not get too comfortable. Things don't feel right. It feels like labor, but it can't be—I'm ten weeks away from my due date."

We called the doctor, who told us to get to the hospital immediately. We took a quick detour to my in-laws' to drop the kids off, then raced to the hospital in a panic.

Sure enough, once I was hooked up to a fetal monitor, we could see that I was definitely in the early stages of labor. I was put on an IV drip of antilabor medicines until all contractions subsided and was sent home the next day with doctor's orders to take it easy—which we knew was a crazy notion in our household.

The doctor wasn't too concerned, but Scott and I were. My previous pregnancies had gone like clockwork. I was one of those women who actually *enjoyed* being pregnant. Aside from the gestational diabetes I'd had while expecting Kendall, which was easy enough to manage, I had been lucky enough to dodge pregnancy adversity pretty much altogether, even avoiding morning sickness for the most part. But when a baby wants to come out early, you start to feel like a walking time bomb, despite medical reassurances.

My lying low meant that Scott had to take on more of the burden around the house, which, contrary to the intended effect, added to my stress. And even though I was trying to take it relatively easy, I ended up back in the hospital with stronger contractions, this time staying for several days while the doctors tried to keep the baby from being delivered prematurely. When I was finally released, it was with physician's orders to remain as still as possible, and a prescription for antilabor drugs that left me jittery and wanting to do anything *but* sit still.

My new prison sentence bucked *all* of my duties to Scott. The thing about a marriage with young children is, it works best if everyone can carry their own weight. Once one spouse or the other has to assume additional burdens, the balance is thrown out of whack and more stresses ensue. We were coping, but I'd be lying if I said we were having a lot of fun. Much of the time we were just trying to get through our days with as little trauma as possible.

Fortunately it wasn't all trauma, drama, and angst. Our kids kept us and each other pretty entertained. One Sunday morning Kyle and Kendall conspired in Kyle's bedroom, insisting that we stay in ours until they called for us. About forty minutes later, they announced we could come to his room. When we opened the door, it set off a chain reaction Rube Goldberg-like happening. They'd attached a string to the door that when opened triggered a switch to come on that turned on a fan that sent feathers flying everywhere. It was so clever— it could only have been more amusing had Graycie been attached to the feathers. It's not an exaggeration to say that such moments preserved Scott's and my sanity.

By the time Graycie took her final dive, I had just started complete bed rest. This meant I had to take a break from tending to Graycie with the exception of special dispensation to allow me to help Scott perform her thrice-daily hydrotherapy, since it was a two-person job. The rest of the time, however, I was to remain immobile. Scott set up the basement playroom for me and the kids. There was a bathroom for vital needs, a cooler with food and drinks, and all the toys and craft projects we needed to get through the day. I was forbidden from getting off the couch as much as possible, which got boring after about an hour. Now *I* was the caged bird, and I didn't like it one bit.

A week into my forced rest, I heard a loud crash from somewhere in the house. I couldn't imagine what had happened— no one was home except Kendall and Kyle and me, and the three of us were virtual prisoners in the basement playroom. I had to go see what the noise was, so against doctor's orders, I crept upstairs. And there, looking as guilty as a gray bird who doesn't blush could look, was Graycie, perched on the edge of a large pot that had up until then housed a five-foot-tall potted palm tree. A palm I'd managed, despite my propensity to kill any houseplant I'd ever encountered, to keep alive for a decade. Somehow she'd opened the cage door, which we must not have closed tightly after her hydrotherapy session, wandered off the cage onto the floor, and walked from the far corner of the dining room, through the kitchen, and into the front hall—a task akin to climbing Everest to such a tiny creature. It probably took her one pass to bite through each stalk of the palm tree; I was surprised she didn't call out, "timber!" That palm tree must've seemed like home to her, and I couldn't help but laugh as I watched her staring at the thing now on the ground, looking as if she was about to say "Uh-oh."

Other than Graycie's tree-cutting adventure, my weeks spent in the basement were pretty uneventful, and the bed rest worked. Two weeks before my due date, the doctor freed me and took me off the miserable terbutalene. Scott and I figured labor would be imminent, and the first night I was allowed to leave the house we decided to take the kids out to dinner since we hadn't been anywhere for two months, and with the new baby due any moment, we probably wouldn't have another chance for a while. We packed up Kyle and Kendall and went to a deli that had opened in a recently built shopping center.

Only one other table was occupied in the restaurant, and soon those people left, so we were the sole remaining patrons. Out of the corner of my eye, I noticed a man walk in and say something to the cashier. Some words were exchanged, and then the man rushed out the door. Right after the door clicked shut, the cashier bolted to the front, locking us in, which I thought was strange. Soon police cars converged upon the place, with sirens wailing and lights ablaze. We'd been so preoccupied with labor pains and finding something our picky kids wanted to eat, and so relieved to finally be out of the house, that a guy had come in and held the place up right under our noses and we barely noticed.

Despite the fact that we were sure I'd go into labor any second, even being in the middle of an armed robbery didn't bring on the birth of our baby, who ended up, after all that bed rest, being a week late. Gillian finally arrived on a fortuitous day, Friday the thirteenth, in the delightful month of May.

~~~~~

Amazingly, we didn't have to take Graycie to the vet's until her annual checkup in November, at which the doctor remarked that she appeared to be in excellent health. Finally, four years into having her, she had been uninjured for a sustained period of time and even seemed to be in decent spirits. Maybe she was being considerate and knew that we didn't need anything more to deal with. If we amortized this period of goodwill over the length of a parrot's life up until then, the hardships ought to balance out, right?

After Thanksgiving, we left Graycie at the vet's while we took a post-holiday family trip with Scott's parents to a Club Med in Florida. The idea was to get a little break from parenting twenty-four/seven—the resort had all sorts of programs for children and day care for the littlest. It sounded great on paper.

However, our kids had no plans to be sloughed off in the day care programs, wise as they were that it meant they weren't going to be vacationing all day with Mom and Dad. They moaned and complained and cried and then almost by design started coming down with every communicable disease available—I'm surprised no one contracted dengue fever. By day two, two kids had already come down with strep, and one, thrush. By day four, on our way to the communal dining hall,

I noticed a woman lean over and throw up into a swimming pool. For some reason that didn't register to me as peculiar—no doubt it merely spurred a flashback to scenes from college, so it appeared entirely within the realm of normalcy.

Once in the dining hall, I saw two more people lurch over and vomit. And within fifteen minutes, Gillian, who was then only six months old, began throwing up as well. Club Med seemed to be experiencing a precursor to those horrid cruise ship viruses that bring an entire vacationing population to its knees. This was the ghost of vacation punishment coming to haunt us yet again.

Scott and I usually try to laugh at adversity, though I can't say we were exactly splitting a gut over this one, as we were piled in a hotel room with cribs, baby supplies, and small children who were desperate for sleep but unable to because of the ongoing trauma.

"Do you think other parents go through all of the stuff that we seem to?" I asked Scott after he got off the phone with the airline. He'd managed to schedule flights home for us—in light of all the throwing up, we were cutting our "vacation" short.

"Let's just focus on what we've got going on here and not worry about what other people are dealing with, okay?"

"I'm just saying . . ."

Our conversation was interrupted by Gillian, who at that moment started gakking yet again.

We spent an arduous night in the hotel with a very sick baby vomiting nonstop, and caught the first flight out in the morning, figuring we might have to hospitalize her for dehydration and would rather do that in our hometown. By that evening Gillian finally started to show signs of recovery. Scott and I tucked all the kids into bed, happy to have dodged a bullet. But around eleven o'clock Kendall emerged from her room in tears, confused and distraught, having thrown up in her bed. We got her cleaned up, changed her sheets, and headed back to our bedroom just in time for Kyle to come out of his room in tears. Rinse, lather, repeat.

At three a.m., I looked at Scott, trying to keep my spirits high.

"Well, at least we're not on the prairie in the 1800s," I said. "I mean, we've got heat in the house and a working washing machine and every time we have to clean another set of sheets, we'll just do it."

Ten minutes later, our washing machine died. At least the furnace didn't fail us.

By dawn, the two of us were as sick as the children. It was the first time since we'd become parents four years earlier that we never got out of bed to go downstairs for a full day. And by the time we were over the bug, which lasted two days, my multitude of laundry was awaiting me, as was the washer repairman. To this day I can't bear to throw out old linens, just in case we might need them in an emergency.

We didn't pick Graycie up from the vet until three additional days after we were scheduled to return from vacation. We simply couldn't deal with her on top of everything else. Luckily, when she got back home she was on her best behavior. For once.

Poor Graycie certainly didn't win the lottery as far as ideal households for a high-maintenance bird. In our home the squeakiest wheels definitely got more grease, and it seemed as if we were operating in triage mode for years at a time. If we were to make a chart of the calm moments in our lives during that period it would likely have a plummeting southward-lurching line. But I figured what goes down must go up, eventually, and in between all the craziness, Scott and I had a lot to be happy about: three clever, adorable, and sweet-spirited children, a great house, a loving family, and lots of supportive friends. We really couldn't complain.

Plus, we were building character, which is a good thing. Isn't it?

~~~~~

We had a lot more character-building in store. Gillian was probably our most energetic child and became quite the skillful climber as a toddler, so my days were spent plucking her off vertical surfaces throughout the home. She was like Baby Spider-Man. I would marvel every time I found Gillian in some gravity-defying location. Preparing meals was a real challenge because Gillian usually chose then to climb into the open dishwasher, wedge herself into the Little Tikes dollhouse like our own version of Gulliver, or mount the kitchen cabinets—the floor-to-ceiling ones that extended well beyond my reach. The bookcases were another favorite. I'd bolt back and forth between stirring pots on the stove, pulling things from the oven, and snatching her as she crawled along the back of the sofa, teetering on the precipice. My daily dinner preparation routine involved my having to put all dining room chairs atop the table upside down, otherwise she would hoist herself up and then crawl at warp speed across the table toward the birdcage, where Graycie was lying in wait to eat small children in her path.

Gillian was fearless and would grin with an enormous

sense of accomplishment with each death-defying climb. At the grocery store there was not a product invented that could contain her in a shopping cart. The Giant provided a stash of kiddie seat belts and I would hoard eight of them, criss-crossing them every which way around and across her body to ensure that she would not stand up in the cart and fall out. Yet still that little Houdini managed to escape. She also liked to peel off whatever clothes were on her body, so usually by aisle three she'd strip off all outerwear, and by aisle six the diaper was missing as well. We got her into gymnastics as soon as she met the age requirement.

I found quite a few parallels between Gillian and Graycie at that time: both loved to climb, both loved to escape (in Graycie's case even if it meant by falling off the cage; in Gillian's, off any surface), and both seemed to derive great pleasure in keeping me on my toes. It's a shame that Gillian's desire to connect with Graycie has always been thwarted by her fear of the beak. And like Graycie, none of the kids always did exactly what we told them to do.

Strong-headed defiance was not in short supply in our home, and at the recommendation of our pediatrician, we sought the sage counsel of a child-rearing book called *1–2–3 Magic,* by Thomas Phelan. We were assured that adherence to the tenets of this book would whip our kids into shape, pronto. The premise was simple: stick to your guns. Give your kid three chances to straighten up, and if at the count of three they choose not to, then they get put in a time-out. This seemed too easy to be effective. But we followed the author's instructions to a *T,* and "That's one. That's two. That's three. Time-out!" became a phrase frequently heard around our home.

Oh lord, the crocodile tears that were shed when the time-out was implemented were unbelievable. You'd think we were torturing them. But while we were following Phelan's very sound advice, Graycie was following the discourse in our home and taking it all in, and before we knew it, our parrot got into the parenting act.

One day, after one of the kids committed a childish transgression, we invoked the fateful words.

"That's one—"

"—Two!" A stern voice came from behind us, interrupting our little punitive dictum.

"Time-out!" Graycie added, skipping right on past "three" and ordering the child to the time-out corner.

Scott and I looked at each other. The kids looked at us. And we all started cracking up, in belly laughs that soon reduced us to tears. The bird had taken it upon herself to put our kids in a time-out. Now *that* we could get used to.

Since that day, any time Graycie hears voices being raised in our home or the kids sassing back at Scott or me, she interjects immediately with "That's one, two, time-out!"

A stern taskmaster, she never lets them get to three.

~~~~~

Not long after Graycie started disciplining the kids, Kyle suddenly lost much of his hearing because of a weird condition called glue ear, in which fluid builds up in the inner ear and settles down for a long winter's nap. This meant an onslaught of doctor's visits with three kids in tow. We were pretty freaked out by it, but the doctors didn't seem to be too concerned. They said often the situation eventually resolved on its own. In the meantime, Kyle had no idea we were talking to him unless we were right up in his face. It was very frustrating for Kyle, who was a gregarious little boy and inclined to ask questions and impart lengthy observations to whoever was nearby all day long. But as his hearing diminished, he withdrew a bit, which was even more concerning.

The doctor put Kyle on steroids to try to help his condition, to no avail. But the drug turned my son into a crazed banshee who wouldn't sleep and was, quite literally, bouncing off the walls. This occurred just in time for me to be socked with a nagging case of pneumonia, which actually had an upside: I finally lost all the baby weight from my last pregnancy. (I'm always looking for that silver lining.)

Although managing our young brood and demanding pets was sucking the energy out of me, when my doctor put *me* on steroids, I turned into Wonder Woman. For four days I became queen of the universe, whipping myself into a cleaning mania (never to occur again), willing and able to tackle all tasks with nary a modicum of effort. I even dared to hold Graycie (those steroids give you an amazing god complex). Day four, however, found me in a fetal position under the comforter, my system having crashed from the 'roids in a bad way.

Over the next six weeks various doctors dispensed one antibiotic after another in an attempt to end Kyle's hearing problem, eventually putting him on vancomycin, considered a "drug of last resort" when it comes to infections. It did nothing. Finally, by spring our ENT decided Kyle needed to have tubes put in his ears. Surgery was hardly a welcome option, but by then we knew if our son was ever going to hear again, we had no choice but to agree to it. So we relented, and the minute he came to in recovery he could hear everything. In fact, he complained about how noisy it was.

Finally we were all on the mend.

~~~~~

That summer I got wise and hired babysitters to watch the kids while I performed mundane errands like grocery shopping. One day while Scott was out of town on business, I arrived home just as I heard on the radio that a tornado had been sighted within several miles of our home. Northern Virginia was hardly tornado alley, and it was almost impossible to take such a threat seriously. But the sky was an ominous, sickly shade of green, so I left the groceries in the car and asked Gina, our babysitter, to settle the kids in the basement. I rounded up the dog and the cats, put Graycie in a cat carrier, and scrambled to find a radio with a battery and a flashlight. We all retreated to our dank, dingy concrete-floored basement, redolent with mildew odors from a flood the previous autumn and several years' worth of cat litter presence. I spread out blankets and handed out the staple food of all mothers (Cheerios—perhaps also the mother of all staple foods), trying to turn the situation into more of a cozy camping experiment than a practice in freaking out over potential impending disaster.

"Okay, gang, let's play Sorry," I said, handing out colored game pieces.

"I want blue!" Kendall said.

"No, *I* want to be blue!" Kyle piped in.

"That's not fair! I called it first!" Kendall retorted.

"I'm red!" Gillian added.

"Wait, I changed my mind. *I* want to be red!" Kendall said.

Ah, a typical day in the life of a mom. But I was happy for any distraction that would get their minds off the impending storm, which arrived within thirty minutes of our settling into the basement.

Our radio chose not to work and the power failed, leaving us in the dark both literally and information-wise, so Gina and I played games by flashlight with the kids while the dog whined and Graycie chewed on her cat carrier trying to escape, occasionally calling out "C'mon, guys!" and sneezing in my husband's voice. Having no experience with tornadoes, we had no idea how long one has to remain hidden, and finally, after about an hour, with the sounds of wind and rain subsiding, we emerged from our cave. We found out we were very lucky; a tornado had indeed touched down on a golf course only blocks from our house, and only ten or so miles away an entire street had been decimated by one.

There was something strangely comforting about having Graycie there to entertain us and keep the kids' minds off their greater fears, simply by spouting off phrases and noises while we huddled in our basement waiting out the storm. She was like a court jester. Kyle, Kendall, Gillian, and I still talk about the day we all hid in the basement with the crazy parrot during a tornado, and thanks to the bird and a fortunate reprieve from Mother Nature, we look back on the day with laughter.

CHAPTER 11

Graycie the Bubble Boy?

The year Graycie turned six was a banner year . . . if we'd been masochists. January presented us with the "blizzard of the century." The kids were five, three and a half, and one and a half, and Scott was in Florida at a trade show when the storm hit. It came fast and furious, with band after band of precipitation that left two feet of snow behind by dawn. Torn between ensuring that my kids were supervised and trying to keep up with the snow shoveling so that we could get out of the driveway as soon as possible to get groceries, I put Kyle in charge of the gang, who remained glued to Disney videos, and I shoveled snow. It was tiring, but I figured D.C. snowstorms were few and far between, so we'd be okay.

The first morning after the storm I spoke by phone with Scott, who mentioned the warm sunshine he was experiencing. No comment. Meanwhile I felt a bit like Lucille Ball at the chocolate factory, unable to keep up with the speeded-up assembly line between the snow, the kids, the dog, the cats, and the parrot, but I was managing fine. That is, until the roof began to leak. First in one spot, then another, then another. Soon it seemed to be leaking in every imaginable area. Water poured in by Graycie's cage at such a rate that I had to put a large trash barrel in the dining room to catch it; melted snow streamed down the sides of two walls in our kitchen like a decorative indoor waterfall—our own uninvited feng shui showpiece—and gushed into the garage as well. It gained entry through airtight (but evidently not watertight) skylights and came in through recessed lighting fixtures.

All in all we had probably ten areas with water flowing into the house, and no way to stop it. I had no intentions of breaking out the mega-ladder and confronting my fear of heights in order to try to figure out how to patch things up. My journalism degree didn't cover water damming, which turned out to be the root cause of the leaks, and I wasn't going to risk a broken neck for *that*.

The region was so inundated with snow that no roads near us were cleared enough to be passable for more than three days. Not that it mattered—I was spending my time trying to catch floodwaters, juggling kids and pets, and watching as ceilings and walls bubbled up until the internal dams broke and another pathway for water flow was opened up. We were in the middle of a water park minus the fun. Graycie was displaced to the middle of the living room, where she would be neglected while I was triaging greater problems. And because I couldn't deal with her being up on her perch, making a mess in the middle of all the other messes, she remained trapped in her cage indefinitely. Not content with her situation, she squawked, loudly, mostly when the kids were napping.

By day three I had to round up the kids to resupply foodstuffs, along with every other human in the greater

D.C. metropolitan area. After slowly cruising through the snowpile-laden Giant parking lot for more than an hour in lane-jockey mode, I finally scored a parking space. When I got inside, the grocery store was mobbed. Shelves had been cleared of most edible ingredients and virtually all staples, and checkout lines stretched up and down aisles. Once we were in line, it took us two hours to get to the frazzled cashier. Always a grocery store commandant who refused to let my kids run roughshod while shopping, for the first time ever I let them play on the undercarriage of the shopping cart. After being cooped up inside for ages, they loved being subversive at the grocery store with Mom's approval. I briefly thought about how awful it must be for Graycie being cooped up in her cage, too, and resolved to find time to give her an opportunity to enjoy a little freedom during this hellish snowstorm aftermath.

Scott got home as soon as the airports opened two days later, and we all had a fabulous time playing and building forts in the snow. I was glad to have Scott home to help deal with the storm's wreckage, and he got to work immediately trying to find roofers to fix our problems, probably secretly wishing he'd stayed in Florida just a bit longer. But it seemed like the worst of winter was over.

A few weeks later, a second storm hit. Another foot of snow fell, which led to more flooding. Scott had to leave for another business trip to Florida, and I made do much as I did the first time, consoling myself with the thought that chances were slim of a third blizzard—this was Washington, after all. We usually got one or two snows a winter, tops. Again, we muddled through and figured out plenty of ways to keep our housebound kids entertained.

Since we first brought Graycie into our home, we've been

aware of the delicate nature of parrots. Anything we've ever read about house-kept birds tends to include endless warnings about how easily they can die. So in addition to *handling* Graycie delicately, we've had to treat her delicately as well, since parrots have fragile constitutions and can drop dead quite unexpectedly. Sometimes I've found it ironic that at the same time I've wanted to throttle our parrot, I've also taken such care to keep her safe from harm. A parrot just isn't as hearty as, say, a Cape buffalo, so I'm constantly worrying about doing something that'll make Graycie sick or exposing her to hazardous things. While Scott will give her a piece of apple after he's bitten from it, I'm of a mind that cross-species diseases can occur (exhibit A: swine flu), so I try to avoid passing on our germs to her. If my parrot is going to be a caged bird, she'll be treated as one, damnit. Sure, I might be verging on paranoid, but better to be safe than sorry, right?

However, sometimes you don't even realize the dangers of what you're handling until far after the fact.

During the winter of much snow, I had to resort to all sorts of crafty indoor activities to keep the kids happy, since preschool was canceled regularly and we couldn't get out to visit any friends because the roads were impassible. Thus we got especially hooked on Sculpey. Sculpey is a fun polymer clay product, somewhat like Play-Doh, only you cook what you make. We spent hours handling the stuff, which came with some warnings on the packaging; I always cleaned everyone's hands thoroughly with alcohol after we played with it, as the warnings had me convinced we were all going to die if I didn't.

One of the main ingredients of polymer clay is PVC, and there have been many rumors about the potential toxicity of PVC over the years. But polymer clay also contains phthalates, which ten years ago we didn't know were as bad for you as we know now. Nowadays they pull baby products off the shelves because of that ingredient. Despite a certain level of ignorance about polymer clay, I knew the first time I cooked the kids' homemade beads, miniature reproductions of food, and little clay animals that we had to be careful with the stuff: the odor as it cooked brought to mind what those fume-choked factories on *The Simpsons* would probably smell like if one could actually visit Springfield and get a whiff of the aroma.

No sooner had we started cooking our little plastic creations than I realized Graycie was perhaps dangerously close to the source of the fumes. So each time we baked Sculpey we moved the parrot to another part of the house, preferably one near an open window, and ventilated the hell out of the kitchen before returning her to her spot.

Considering it was the dead of winter, I was faced with a decision: we either abandon our favorite craft project (one all the kids could do and enjoy for a decent stretch of time) or risk the parrot's freezing to death next to an open window (her source of fresh air) or keeling over from fumes. We finally decided to give up Sculpey for the bird. The kids were disappointed, but by that point I had concerns that it wasn't so healthy for *anyone* in our house to be inhaling those fumes, so in a way Graycie was just protecting our health by default. This experience made me grateful for my little canary in the coal mine, but it also made me wonder how paranoid one must be when housing something with a delicate constitution. Should Graycie become the Bubble Boy? Make that the Bubble Bird? Our house was seeming more and more hazardous by the minute.

We got yet *another* foot of snow that winter, this time with

Scott at home, thankfully. The roof leaked in so many places we lost count, while also losing morale. You can dump only so many buckets of floodwater before despair sets in. Roof problems were so common in our area from the winter of our discontent that we were unable to find an available roofer for months, so we dealt with the leaks on and off during every rainstorm that spring as well. Graycie lived in a cage-on-the-move during this period, and I think she actually enjoyed the change of scenery; unfortunately, the constant moving expanded her mess zone exponentially, as we could no longer confine it to one corner of the house. I got so tired of seeing the telltale water bubbles erupt from my ceiling that I finally stopped looking up.

The blizzards were followed by such frequent bouts of strep in our household (including insidious, and very serious, strep-related medical problems for Scott) that by spring the doctor put the entire family—plus the dog and cats—on antibiotics at the same time, with the hope of finally eradicating the infections in our household. We were declared strep-free that summer after the longest spring I can remember. Only Graycie was disappointed when things finally got back to normal and she was back in her corner.

CHAPTER 12

Why Is Muffy Smiling?

Scott continued to travel a lot the year after the blizzard, and in October he went on a business trip right after we began a project to replace the rotting fence surrounding our house on its corner lot. Our house was adjacent to a busy intersection, and our property seemed vulnerable without a sturdy fence as a buffer.

The night after Scott left, I heard a carload of rowdy partiers with music blasting pull up to the construction Dumpster near the fence and dump a bunch of empty bottles, which shattered the quiet night air. I'd have thought nothing more of it except that a minute later, our power went out. A glance out my front window revealed that all of the neighbors' homes were lit up just fine. Our neighborhood frequently lost power due to aged power lines, and the county had been trying to stop this problem from recurring, but never had we been the only house left without lights.

So there I was, at eleven o'clock at night, with three children tucked into bed and no working telephone (since they were powered by electricity), jittery and worried that the outage was somehow linked to the group of carousers who'd just been dumping things right outside my bedroom window. My vivid imagination was getting the better of me, and I started envisioning gory scenes from every slasher flick I'd ever seen. Finally I calmed myself down enough to shut off all light switches and retreated to bed.

A word about me and sleeping children. Our youngest, Gillian, was so averse to sleep that by day she refused to nap, regularly passing out in her high chair midbite from exhaustion, a windup toy needing another winding. Sometimes she'd simply slump to sleep while sitting in my lap. So once I had my kids asleep, I did not take kindly to anyone or anything that dared wake them up. Sleep had become more precious to me than just about anything, barring my actual kids themselves. One of my parenting hall of shame moments occurred during that time, when I'd finally gotten Gillian to sleep one evening. Many nights she'd somehow snap awake the instant I left the room, so I knew I had to slip out unnoticed. On that particular evening, I slithered down the side of the crib, hoping my aging knees wouldn't creak too loudly on the way down, until I was flat on the carpet on my belly. And then ever so slowly I did the commando crawl, backward, inching my way gradually out of the room, hooking my finger under the bottom edge of the door and drawing it closed before I finally slipped into the hallway. There's a reason sleep deprivation is used as a means of torture: it works. Clearly it had fogged my brain from entirely rational behavior. But you can see why I didn't want anybody waking up unbidden in my house, ever.

At about two in the morning, Beau, who usually slept

through everything, woke me with her barking. Between barks she was letting forth a menacing growl I'd never heard from her before. This was the dog to whom any burglar would only have had to offer up a juicy steak and she'd have welcomed them warmly into the house. Hell, they could've given her a platter of dog poo and she'd have wagged with glee and handed over the keys.

Every attempt to shush her failed. At that point I was worried that she'd wake up my brood for the next several hours, and I was already so on edge my psyche couldn't deal with an all-nighter. But Beau clearly meant business—her fur was standing on end on her back, and her face was pointing to a wall of windows at the back of the house where I saw a man standing on my back deck, silhouetted in the moonlight. My heart pounding, I realized I was still stuck in a house with no phone and had no idea what to do, with a strange man right outside my window.

Graycie chose that moment to start yelling at the dog. In my voice. Loudly.

"Shhhhhh! Beau! Stop barking!"

That was just what I needed, for the bird to let the burglar know someone was home *and* awake—someone he could slash to death with the razor blade extenders he no doubt wore on his fingers and then eat with fava beans and a glass of chianti.

I stood, frozen in place with fear, staring at the stranger hunched over on my back deck. After about twenty seconds, I noticed his toolbox. And then his hard hat. And then I could just make out a logo emblazoned on the front of it: VEPCO. He was from the electric company, working on the power outage. He hadn't wanted to ring the bell and wake us up in the middle of the night, so he'd gone out back to work on my utility box without advance notice. In the process of sparing me lost sleep, he took about ten years off my life, in collaboration with my dog and my parrot.

~~~~~

Soon after being "protected" by my barkaholic Lab, I was leafing through an issue of *People* magazine and stopped on a funny image of a dog, distorted through a fish-eye lens, with the headline "Why Is Muffy Smiling?"

Muffy's scruffy mug was indeed smiling up at me; she certainly appeared to be a happy dog. I read on and found out why: because Muffy was high!

Turns out there was a vet who just happened to have a practice nearby (with a satellite office in Beverly Hills) who had started treating dogs plagued by allergy-induced obsessive compulsive behavior with Prozac, and seeing great results. It was sort of like medical marijuana for mutts. *What a novel idea,* I thought: keep the dog stoned enough that she didn't feel compelled to self-mutilate. This was during Prozac's early days, when it was considered not only a wonder drug but also mother's little helper. I knew a slew of peers who were using the stuff as a maternal coping tool, and they all seemed eerily chipper in a Stepford Wives kind of way. Was this the cure-all, even for an itch-crazed Labrador? By then we were so desperate with Beau's problems, we were ready to try anything. And while we were at it, maybe we could slip a little mickey into Graycie's kibble. . . .

I will admit it gave us pause that this specialist not only had an office in the most expensive bedroom community of D.C., but one with a 90210 zip code as well. His office overhead alone would surely tack on a hefty price tag for his services.

But Muffy *was* smiling, and how could we put a price on happiness for our pets? And by default, us? After all, happy pet, happy owner, right?

I made an appointment and Scott and I met with the Doc Hollywood, who was a very polished, well-groomed fellow who looked, well, like he had an office in Beverly Hills (along with a Learjet to get him there). From the minute we arrived, we were completely out of our element. We were used to dealing with a folksy down-home vet who got his hands dirty, not one who looked like he had his hands manicured.

Our regular dog vet usually just sent us home with another tube of ointment for Beau with each allergy-related health disaster she experienced. The fancy vet upped the ante big-time, and smacked us with a dog maintenance regimen that was obscenely overwrought and had us catering nonstop to our dog's medical needs disproportionately to the rest of ours. Yet we adhered to it obligingly because we loved that dog, allergies and all, and we saw this as a last-ditch effort to help Beau enjoy a somewhat normal life. We felt that we owed it to her to give it a try.

First up: weekly allergy shots. Testing revealed that Beau was allergic to basically anything that was in the atmosphere: dust, mites, pollen of all kinds, molds, mildews, leaves, flowers, grass, fleas, and flea dirt. Oh, and dog food and almost every filler therein, particularly corn, beef, and chicken. We also had to have a costly batch of custom serum prepared for her host of allergies. I nominated Scott for the job of shot giver; I'll clean up bird poop, but injecting the dog with needles? No way!

Next came the hundred-buck-a-month Prozac prescription. I often tried to get Scott to pick that up as well, because I didn't want anyone thinking my name was Beau Gardiner when the pharmacist announced the Prozac prescription was ready. Scott could have cared less, but when I'd have to pick it up I always felt compelled to say—loudly—"It's for my dog!" As if the pharmacist or any customers cared.

In addition to the shots and the uppers, Beau had a daily regimen of vitamin supplements and skin oils to enhance the health of her coat, prednisone to counteract the itch, antibiotics for the infections, and ointments for the fungi, all of which we had to stuff down her gullet, apply to her paws or ears, or inject into her hide. When Beau saw us coming she'd hide in a closet, knowing what she was about to be subjected to.

To top it all off, I had to prepare homemade dog food, which consisted of steamed rice and pureed canned vegetables, twice a day. I also had to bathe the dog daily, to keep the myriad threatening allergens from settling on her fur. Considering I was already used to hosing down the birdcage in any sort of weather, the dog-washing chore hardly fazed me, except that Beau was extremely uncooperative during the process, and I constantly ended up soaked. And of course no one (okay, maybe Barney and Arthur) was minding my kids while I was out making the world safe for my allergic pet, or Graycie, who would take this opportunity to wander off the cage, prompting the kids to come running to me to report on the wayward parrot.

Clearly this optimistic vet didn't realize that in the coping department we were barely hanging on by a thread and didn't need another ultra-high-maintenance pet regimen to tip us over the edge. Yet we did our best to follow his suggestions— it really was that or put the dog down, and we couldn't do that and sleep at night. So Scott and I divvied up Beau-related tasks as best we could and tried to remind ourselves and each other that we were doing the right thing and all the effort was well worth it.

Within a couple of months, we saw a substantial improvement in Beau. She certainly smelled vastly better. She'd also lost weight, thanks to her vegetarian diet, and she was no longer scratching until she bled. But she was always, always, always stoned. She was a doggie in a daze, wandering around looking like she might walk into the wall that just jumped out at her. She was probably seeing flying purple people eaters coming at her, too. Sadly, I feel like we *never* reclaimed Beau's personality, lost as it was first to obsessive behaviors to tame the itch/pain of allergies, then to the psychotropic meds we were pumping her full of.

Beau wasn't the only one in our household undergoing a medical intervention at that time. I'd spent much of my "free time" that year seeking medical answers myself for a mystery ailment that no one could seem to figure out. Finally I was diagnosed with Lyme disease, which by then was entrenched in my central nervous system. I had been so chronically exhausted that I could barely keep my head up at the dinner table by six in the evening, and my joints ached as if I was an octogenarian. I'd also been enveloped in a mental fog so thick I almost didn't realize it had happened, it had come on so gradually. Of course for a long time I'd attributed this to my chaotic life. Who wouldn't be exhausted from dealing with what we had going on? And I was in my thirties—things stop working so well right about then, right? But I'd eventually gotten to the point where lugging a baby in one arm and a laundry basket in the other up a flight of stairs was an undertaking so exhausting I had to lie down for twenty minutes afterward just to regain my strength, and I knew that couldn't be normal.

It was a blessing to finally have an infectious disease specialist tell me I wasn't just neurotic, that there was a reason I'd been losing my memory and experiencing at least forty other symptoms that were interfering with my ability to function. Finally, treatment was going to happen for *me,* as well. The doctor put me on oral antibiotics, which at first made me even sicker. But this wasn't uncommon, and soon I started to feel a little more energetic, though still not myself. Ultimately the doctor decided I needed to go on IV antibiotics, so for two months over the holidays and into the new year, I spent at least an hour each morning and night tethered to a bag of fluid that was gradually infusing life back into me.

Scott and I pretty much neglected Graycie for that entire year, but the kids adored her and would go near the cage and talk with her often. Of course they never went too close, what with that evil beak of hers; I longed for the day when our kids would actually be able to handle the parrot beyond the buffer zone. As the kids grew older and were able to interact with Graycie more and more, I found it funny how they took for granted that we had this resident parrot who spoke like us throughout the day, as if that was a mainstream occurrence in people's lives. Thankfully, during my battle with Lyme disease, Grayce was on autopilot and kept us entertained. She'd learned the high points of the song "Happy Birthday" and uncannily sang them precisely on each of our birthdays (and, amazingly, on no other days). She also began uttering the words "Merry Christmas" that year, and always when things seemed to be especially frustrating, she would find the perfect time to inject humor by saying or doing something entirely amusing. It was definitely a year of challenges, but with a little elbow grease, a few hefty doses of meds, and a lot of laughter, we all managed to pull through.

CHAPTER 13

The Gallic Shrug and the End of an Era

After my Lyme disease had been treated, we entered a period of normalcy. Graycie was generally pleasant and enjoyed those moments when we could find the time to hold her. Which weren't frequent. Caring for her wasn't like taking a dog for a walk, which could double as a family activity plus exercise. Time with Graycie meant time with Graycie, period. If I held the parrot, it meant I wasn't playing with my kids, fixing meals, doing laundry, cleaning the house, or, god forbid, exercising or sleeping. Or sewing Halloween costumes, making overachiever-mom birthday cakes (of which I was quite guilty and for which I occasionally pulled all-nighters), organizing birthday parties, hosting playdates, washing the dog, cooking dog food, or trekking off to any number of classes and activities with my children.

But Scott and I felt that we'd begun to get a handle on our lives a little bit. For one thing, our pets had finally become relatively manageable, which simplified life enormously. I even spent that summer getting all three kids down for naps at the same time, so that I could lounge once again on a floating chair in our swimming pool, reading books, which seemed like such a luxurious indulgence. Things were going smoothly, so why rock the boat, right?

One night in early June, Scott and I were relaxing and watching the eleven o'clock news when we saw an impassioned plea for locals to volunteer to host foreign exchange students. Some organization had a group of French students slated to arrive in a week's time and hadn't found nearly enough host sponsors, and without volunteer hosts coming forward, the trip would be off, the kids' hopes dashed.

I turned to Scott. "I always wished I'd done something like that."

Since he'd lived overseas when he was a child, he greatly appreciated the value of foreign travel, and empathized with the kids' plight immediately.

"You think we should host a student?" he asked.

"I guess it'd be interesting to get to know someone from another country. Maybe it would launch a lifelong friendship, and we'd go to visit their home in France someday."

"Yeah, it could be fun," Scott agreed.

"Plus, it would be a nice gesture," I said. "Besides, how much work could it be?"

Indeed.

Clearly we had a pattern of taking on more than we thought we were taking on, and this undertaking was to be no exception. My brother Gene's wife, Diane, one of my dearest friends who lived just minutes away, just shook her head at me when I told her the news about our upcoming houseguest over dinner a few nights later.

"You are crazy," she said. "Don't you think you have enough going on in your lives without having to deal with this?"

My good friend Stacey, whose older two kids were close friends with Kyle and Kendall, agreed.

"I'm all for traveling and stuff," she said. "But this is going to be like having another kid you're responsible for!"

I don't know if we deluded ourselves or if we just couldn't shirk our perpetual inclination to help out, but whatever the reason, a week later we found ourselves welcoming Pierre, a sullen, awkward teen and master of the French shrug, that expression of ambivalence for which an entire nation is known. From the moment he arrived, Pierre made sure to minimize the amount of time he spent in our presence, and instead holed up in the guest bedroom (which was actually my messy sewing room and was piled high with fabric, supplies, unfinished projects, and patterns galore—just what every teenage boy would hope for). Pierre might well have been disappointed that he got stuck in a household with three little kids and a host of animals to which he seemed most unreceptive. He disliked when the smelly dog repeatedly stuck her snout in his crotch (I can't say that I blamed him), and didn't particularly love the shrieking parrot (and children) who awoke him daily before his own body clock ever did. Perhaps he resented that some of the more studly French boys in his group were paired off in households with fresh-faced, lithe American teen girls. Who knows? The bottom line is, Pierre wasn't particularly thrilled about bunking down with us, and the shrug didn't do much to mask that impression.

"Pierre, would you like some juice?" I'd ask at breakfast.

To which he replied with a shrug and a grunt.

"Pierre, would you like to go into Washington to see some museums?"

Grunt. Shrug.

"Pierre, would you like to join us for a weekend at the beach?"

Shrug.

"Pierre, would you like to take back your entire plan to be an exchange student in the U.S.?" I once asked jokingly, certain that his command of English was not strong enough for him to understand. I was right, and he simply shrugged.

We'd been unaware that hosting our student involved more than providing a bed with clean sheets and some meals and showing him around, teaching him about our country. It also meant shuttling him to and from an extensive list of daily activities as well as group social gatherings at night. It even entailed having forty rowdy French teens and their hosts over for a swimming party in our pool. (As a side note, we had no idea how much trouble teenagers could get into in a swimming pool.)

More than anything else, Pierre's disdain for our parrot was palpable. When Graycie shrieked, he would glance at her with one of those searing looks people save for their archenemies. It was almost as if he glared in French.

By the time our guest's six-week stay had ended, we were ready to send our temporary teenager back home. Sure, we'd bonded, but not exactly in a let's-visit-next-summer kind of way. It was a learning experience, but not one we planned to repeat anytime soon.

The following June, Scott and I were up late watching the news when we saw an impassioned appeal by the very same exchange group, begging locals to host French students who would be arriving in a week's time. Didn't we feel like suckers, having fallen for the ploy that was obviously how they found hosts year in and year out? It would be a good decade before we hosted a French foreign exchange student again (of course we gave it another shot: we're the ultimate suckers!), but luckily that experience ended up being so wonderful, it made up for our pet-hating, anticonversationalist houseguest in spades.

~~~~~~

While hosting Pierre wasn't the most rewarding experience, it had taught us something that led to a major transition. Having hosted a stranger for almost an entire summer in our house, we were acutely aware that our home didn't adequately accommodate houseguests. Plus, with the kids getting bigger, our once seemingly spacious house began to feel awfully small. The towering ceilings provided a lot of open air above us, but we were lacking useable space, particularly where it mattered, with bedrooms, bathrooms, and closets.

I'm like Graycie in that I don't take kindly to change, so while I relished the idea of more space, I didn't embrace the notion of uprooting, even if it was just to a community twenty minutes away. It didn't help matters that as we looked at houses, we again became dismayed with the uniformity of house designs in the Northern Virginia area. The region seemed plagued with old-school center hall colonials, ramblers, and split-levels, and all the new construction lacked character, mature trees, and the slightest hint of privacy. We didn't want to give up the things we loved about our house simply to gain a closet or a bathroom.

We'd been spoiled living in our gorgeous contemporary

with a swimming pool, although we vowed never to have one again, as the burden of responsibility of having ten thousand gallons of water in one's backyard became more and more clear the older the kids became. When they were little, "all" we had to worry about was our children drowning—worrisome enough, even though we'd added a tall wrought-iron fence to keep unwelcome toddlers away from danger after having ditched the pool alarm, which went off whenever the wind blew or a leaf dropped into the water. But as the kids grew up, they became rowdy risk-takers, doing crazy tricks off the diving board and sides of the pool. When one of Kyle's friends knocked a tooth out on a raft handle while horsing around, it was a wake-up call. It was bad enough to have to call a mom to tell her that her daughter was coming home minus a tooth (at least it was a baby tooth, but it hadn't even been loose). We didn't want to have to deal with worse.

The more we looked at houses, the more we hated everything we saw. And the more we realized we were weary with living in suburban sprawl, with its inherent overdevelopment, burgeoning traffic problems, and overpopulation. Life seemed to be an endless competition for parking spaces and bathroom lines at family events advertised in the *Washington Post*. Road jockeying had risen to the level of blood sport on the highways. Besides which, we weren't even comfortable allowing our kids to go out on our street to ride bikes unattended. It seemed our children were living like caged birds, just like their beloved parrot.

"You know, when I moved to D.C., I loved being near the city," I said to Scott one day a few weeks into our search. "But we actively *avoid* the city now. Why are we even living here anymore?"

It was true—we used to go out of our way to attend events in the District, and would take the Metro to museums and monuments. Now, the reality of doing so with three little kids just made it something with which we were disinclined to bother. On the other hand, we were rooted by family to the area—Scott's entire immediate family lived nearby, as did Diane and Gene—so it was hard to imagine making the break. But Scott ran his business out of our home, and he could move it anywhere, and I was a stay-at-home mom, so no job tied me down. Ultimately it felt like the right time to branch out and see what else was out there. We started considering new locations.

"California would be awesome!" I suggested, to which Scott rolled his eyes and shook his head vigorously.

"What about Arizona?" I asked. I'd been to the state only once, just before that little salmonella episode. Perhaps I recalled it fondly simply because it remained a beacon of rest and relaxation in a less-than-peaceful life. Plus, the cabana boys who brought me fruity drinks while I lingered in the pool were awfully memorable. *That* I could live with.

"Are you crazy?" Scott said, pulling me out of my poolside fantasy. "You know how hot it gets in Arizona?"

"It's dry heat!" I said in defense, to no avail.

"Jen, I want to be within driving distance of my family."

Our moving criteria was pretty limiting. Anything north of D.C. was too cold. Anything past easy road-trip distance was out. So we started exploring Virginia and, to our happy surprise, discovered we loved the landscape in the center of the state, with the majestic foothills of the Blue Ridge Mountains always hovering nearby. In our travels we'd been drawn to the English countryside, and Virginia's back roads had a similar appeal (albeit substantially hotter in the summertime), with stacked stone and split-rail fences and grazing horses, happy cows, and lazy sheep.

I hated the idea of saying goodbye to our many friends, all the people who had gone through those early childhood years with us—friends who were like fellow combat veterans with whom we'd shared so many highs and lows. And I loathed the notion of upsetting Graycie's contented little world again, since she had finally settled somewhat happily into our family. I also dreaded discovering what else we could find for Beau to be allergic to in another part of the state. Last, I feared giving up my hairstylist. I mean come on—once you find someone who can do your hair, that person is supposed to go with you to the grave.

Eventually the pro column outweighed the cons, and within the year, we'd loaded up a moving van and our gang headed for central Virginia, trading postage stamp lots and bumper-to-bumper traffic for pastures and horses and stars in the night sky. For a good year or two I continued to road-trip to Northern Virginia for hair appointments, for vet appointments for Graycie (we loved Dr. Stahl and hated to give him up), and to get my shopping fix, but for the most part I was glad our town had been mercifully and entirely bypassed by the retail development monster that had taken hold of the D.C. area.

During our return trip from Scott's parents' home the following Thanksgiving, it was officially cemented into our minds that we had moved to a rural area, far from shopping malls and other urban distractions. As we rounded a traffic circle just about half an hour from home, we saw in the distance the flashing lights of a police car. It was late and the kids needed to get to bed, so we were dismayed that there was a roadblock deterring our route. Then we got a bit closer and realized why we were stopped: a herd of cattle had broken loose and were milling about in the dark along the two-lane road that led us home. The kids were thrilled to be up close and personal with bumper-to-bumper cattle. Yep, we weren't in Kansas anymore.

CHAPTER 14

Home Sweet Home

My husband grew up overseas and moved a number of times when he was young, and so I think he is now a bit like a tethered falcon, often longing to spread his wings and see where the thermals will take him. But he's been kept grounded by me and my reluctance to pack up households, children, pets, lives, and the comforts of home and take off for the great unknown. Even though I suggested moving clear across the country, I'm too much of a wimp to actually do it without being forcefully plucked from my home and dropped down elsewhere. In fact I was pretty proud that I was able to uproot from living comfortably in the D.C. area for some fifteen years when we chose to seek a smaller town in which to raise our children.

Scott and I bought a lot in a small community with the intention of building a house to suit our needs, but this meant living in temporary digs indefinitely. When we road-tripped to our new town to search for a house to rent, we couldn't find anything that would accommodate our family of five, an aging dog, two elderly cats, the parrot, my husband's office, and a warehouseful of his company's samples and products (with a stockpile of nearly fifteen years' worth of T-shirts, greeting cards, posters, and other items that his company designed and licensed onto such products, we could have practically opened a store). And when we did find places that would accommodate our needs for space, we found they'd be lacking in another area. I remember looking at a run-down, dank, and gloomy vicarage for rent that was plenty spacious but gave off the creepy vibe that resident (and hostile) ghosts fully occupied all nooks and crannies therein. My husband, never quite attuned to those little details that I think women pick up on instinctively, was ready to sign on the dotted line.

"This place is great! We can fit everything in here!" he enthused. "Plus there's lots of property. The kids can run around. Beau will love it!"

We'd been used to the minuscule lots of Northern Virginia where you can see into your neighbor's bathroom and vice versa, so sure, space was appealing.

"This place gives me the willies," I said, looking around with dismay at the peeling paint, linoleum floors, and sagging walls. "No way in hell you're going to get me to live here without a lifetime supply of Prozac. And I'm not taking Beau's."

We continued to look for housing, to no avail.

By some crazy coincidence, a family we'd met at the beach the previous summer when our little girls had befriended each other over seashells and sand castles had also moved to our new town, right into the house next door to our lot. But before we even had a chance to move, they'd decided to relocate farther out in the country, and wanted to sell their house fast. They offered us a remarkable deal to purchase their home, with an added incentive: they would cover half our mortgage for six months if we couldn't sell it when it came time to move into the home we were about to build.

So after selling our house in Fairfax in six easy hours, we were facing buying a house for nine months and having to flip it pronto, or else be broke, pronto, and if it sold too soon, possibly having to find yet another temporary home in which to camp out, pronto. This was a tough scenario for a risk-averse person who won't even grant a handshake when casually saying to someone, "I betcha a hundred bucks." But the house fit all our needs (except that need to avoid bankruptcy), and in a matter of weeks we were the proud owners of a house we never wanted to own, knowing full well that the minute we moved in we were essentially going to have to put it on the market. It was a daunting prospect, made even more unnerving by the presence of kids who weren't known for being neat and orderly, and of course that contingent of mess-making house pets. But the house fit all our needs, with the added bonus of being located right next door to our future abode, so we took the deal and started packing.

The kids were particularly concerned about moving the pets. The cats meowed the entire trip in the car but, after disappearing for a day or two behind all the moving boxes in our temporary home, seemed to adjust without a hitch. Beau immediately loved the place, especially the woods and fields nearby. And as soon as we set up Graycie's cage and put her in it, she let out a loud and long catcall, so we knew she'd be fine.

Graycie was fairly happy in her temporary little breakfast nook overlooking dense woods. Sometimes she would watch delicate blue herons alight from a nearby pond, winging right past the bank of windows she was gazing out of. This only compounded the guilt I felt as I grumbled about her cage mess while she no doubt longed to be as free as those birds. But every minute we spent in that house I was aware that I needed to keep it in open house–ready condition so we could sell it in a flash.

Over that long winter we appreciated the benefits of living next door to our home-building project. We were able to oversee construction crews, bribe them with pizza dinners and hot dogs, and once prevent the driver of a cement truck from dumping its contents into a grove of preserved hardwoods out front—despite its being cordoned off with signs reading "Keep Off"—before he turned our designated front yard into a parking lot. The house was finished on time and with very few mishaps, and we were ecstatic with the results.

But we had to sell that darned other house, and sell it to people who would be our next-door neighbors. So while we wanted to be selective about who purchased it, we also felt a bit desperate. As luck would have it, nine months after moving in, we sold it to a lovely older couple just as we prepared to move into our new home. And as workers started planting the shrubbery and trees that would dot the landscape of our new yard, the kids and I lugged laundry basket loads of belongings from next door into the new place, while Scott supervised and helped the movers with the big things.

Building our own home gave us the luxury of keeping features we loved about our previous home while rectifying some of its shortcomings, including where in the house we would relegate Graycie to keep her near all the action with the least ancillary mess. Because aside from the mess within the cage itself, the periphery around it is also a trashed zone. Parrots throw their food while they eat it, and generally the foods they eat are sticky and messy: grapes, berries, bananas, and such.

In our first two houses, Graycie's cage went where we could accommodate it, which meant it wasn't set up for the slop, and the surrounding area ended up bloodied and stickified. She hated living in the basement of our first home. In the next house, while there was plenty of space, it still wasn't designed to buffer the mess. We came up with the brilliant idea of buying huge rectangles of hard plastic sheeting to protect the walls from the food stains and the projectile poops (have I mentioned that parrots can shoot that stuff pretty far if they want to?), and in theory the Lucite sheets helped matters, but they were yet one more thing to have to perpetually keep clean and were impossible to lug in and out of the house for washing.

When we built our current house, we decided we were going to address this ongoing problem. We added a four-foot by four-foot section to the footprint of the house in the corner where our living room and dining room meet in order to accommodate the birdcage. The design upgrade added roughly five thousand dollars to the cost of building (the things we do for our pets). This area was to be tiled in, thus easily wipeable, and voilà, life would be much, much simpler. As if that weren't enough, we designed a mudroom with a shower so that I could wash the cage with warm water. No more poopsicles while washing the cage outside in the winter!

Such well-thought-out plans.

Though I maintained that the standard-issue shower insert wasn't large enough to accommodate the birdcage, Scott insisted it would be fine. Now, my husband hails from serious do-it-yourself stock. His father, a hugely talented woodworker, is seldom without a tape measure and a toolbox. So far be it from me to question any Gardiner man's measuring skills, especially because my own are laughable. Even *I* don't trust my own measuring ability, and to this day I'm paralyzed by simple mathematical equations. But I did know from years of dealing with the messy cage that our intended space for indoor cleaning wasn't big enough.

"You know this isn't gonna fly," I said, pointing to the mudroom shower. No bird pun intended. "No way is that cage going to fit in here."

At which point my husband whipped out his tape measure like a seasoned veteran, extending it here, minimizing it there.

"See, my numbers mesh perfectly with the sizes we're looking at," he assured me.

I just shook my head. "I'm telling you, the cage isn't gonna fit."

Turns out the shower insert was just about the exact size of the birdcage, which meant you couldn't maneuver it when trying to wash the thing, and blasts of poop would fly all over the room when using it if we went to the trouble of trying to wedge the thing into the shower to use it for its intended purpose. But all was not lost, as the shower instead became "the dog shower."

The tiled-in cage area? Well . . . again, it was a great idea, which we naively thought was worth an extra few thousand bucks in order to vastly minimize the mess and thus our work cleaning it up. And it would have, except that African grays are extremely pliable. These birds can stretch and reach and get into all sorts of trouble. So Graycie soon learned that she could extend just far enough while standing on the cage to chew the drywall off the corners of the wall, and while she was at it, she could get that power beak of hers right beneath the edge of the tile and dig it out of the wall if she turned her beak just so this way and then that way. By the time we realized she'd been excavating away, our Italian tiles had deep troughs dug beneath them. And the decorative plates on the walls around the corner from the cage? Well, if her cage is in the position we planned for it to occupy, then she can just reach around and pull the plates off the wall, causing them to shatter. Which she has done, to her immense satisfaction.

Clearly we learned all these lessons the hard way. It would take us a few more years to give in to the inevitable, pulling her cage a few feet out and away from the cleverly tiled walls, right in the path of all who walk between the living room and dining room, where if you're not careful she'll reach right out and bite your shirt. Or your flesh.

But overall, building a house to suit our needs made life so much easier, and it didn't take much for us to no longer question our decision to move. That first autumn in our home, we'd heard there was to be a spectacular Leonid meteor shower. Having lived in a metropolitan suburb for years, to us stars were more of a concept than a reality due to light pollution. The night of the meteor shower, I peered out the window and couldn't believe what was happening. Despite the late hour, I rounded up the rest of the family and we all grabbed our sleeping bags and lay down on the back deck, snuggled together to stay warm. For a couple of hours in the black of night we were bombarded with brilliant shooting stars that seemed destined for our backyard, they were so close and so bright. It was magical. And we knew for certain that we'd made the right decision to move to the country.

~~~~~

About a year after we moved in, I finally felt settled. The kids were happy in school, I'd found a growing group of friends to supplant those I'd left behind, and our crazy bird was enjoying her special spot in the house. It was precisely at this point that Scott started getting the itch to spend some time overseas.

He came home one day after discovering some miracle software that was going to free him up to conduct his business anywhere. This was right around the turn of the century, before technology had gotten to the point that it has now, where many people can do that effortlessly. Back then it was still an innovative concept.

"I've got great news!" he announced, beaming.

"What?" I couldn't imagine what he had to tell me, but he looked so thrilled I guessed it had to be something I'd be pleased about, too.

"Well, you'd better sit down and I'll explain." My excitement instantly wavered. I get really nervous when people tell me I have to sit down before they can tell me something. So my guard was raised.

He launched into how, thanks to his new discovery, we could just up and move anywhere, if only for a year or two. It would be great!

My face turned ashen. We'd just settled down. We had our lovely new home, which we hadn't even had a chance to trash too much yet. I was still in that optimistic phase where I wiped fingerprints off the walls regularly and polished the countertops clean with Windex on a daily basis.

"But what about our *house*?"

"Easy—we'll swap with a family from another country. We'll move into their house; they'll move into ours."

Swap. All our things. With strangers who could trash our home before we got the chance to do it in our own way. Or who could accidentally burn the place down. And we could move someplace where we'd know no one and not speak the language and the girls—who still hadn't resumed sleeping through the night due to the anxiety of the move—would be waking us at three a.m. until we were retirees. (This is probably a good time to mention that when Scott's family moved overseas when he was young, the renters turned the main ground-level floor into a repository for motorcycles and left motor oil stains all over the floor that required industrial-strength cleaning to eradicate.)

"Ummm . . . I'm not gonna say an all-out no to this, but let's just say I'm not a fan of the idea," I said, looking down at the floor, knowing how disappointed he'd be with my unadventurous spirit. "I'll be happy to put it up to a family vote, but I can't understand why we'd do this when we are finally feeling settled."

The fact is, I knew people who'd gone overseas for a year, and usually they spent a good year in advance preparing to go, spent most of the year abroad trying to get used to living in a new environment, and then just when they got acclimated, they returned home to have to try to resettle again. As much as I love to travel abroad for short periods of time, I really couldn't see the appeal of leaving then.

When the kids came home from school that day, Scott had everyone sit down for the big powwow.

"Sounds cool, let's go," my son said.

Typical male. *Just throw me some food, give me a pair of boxers, and point the way.*

The girls were a bit more tepid about the notion. "What would we do with all of our pets?" Kendall asked.

"We'd farm them out with family and friends!" Scott said, as if we were lending out a set of yard tools.

"Who in their right mind would want our pets?" I asked. "I mean, *we* can barely manage them all. They're a lot of work."

"Not to worry," he insisted. "It'll all work out."

Typical male. *Just look at the big picture, don't focus on the minutiae.*

The girls weren't too keen on that idea.

"But we love our pets!" they both cried. And they did. Our pets are our good friends; we talk to them, we joke with them, we play with them. We wouldn't ditch a good friend in such a cavalier manner, so how could we do so with them?

"Okay, fine, we'll take them with us," Scott said, thinking that concession had settled that sticking point.

"But Graycie—we can't bring her," I said. "There are strict rules about transporting birds across borders. I bet you couldn't find a country that would let you just bring a parrot in without a lengthy quarantine."

"Yeah, Graycie would have to go to jail again!" Gillian cried. "She'd die!" No repeating birdie Gitmo for our feathered friend.

"Well, she can go live with someone for the time we're gone!" he said.

I could see tears welling in the girls' eyes. They were shaking their heads back and forth.

"And what about our stuff?" Kendall asked.

"Your stuff? It'll stay here!" Scott was still trying to paint this rosy picture, but the storm clouds were creeping in despite his best efforts.

"But we want to bring our stuff along!"

"Fine, fine. You can bring it with you." His voice had risen an octave. He was clearly becoming irate as he watched his grandiose plans crumbling before his very eyes.

"But what about our furniture?"

Now, I've always joked that my husband would skin the cats if someone needed a coat. He's a generous soul and very comfortable sharing just about everything. The kids and I are less inclined to risk our things being ruined, at the hands of strangers, no less. "The people who stay here will use it."

Cue the look of horror on their faces at the idea of strangers occupying their space, using their things at their disposal. I of course was envisioning flea or head lice infestations. Bedbugs if we were really screwed.

"Even our *beds?*" Kendall asked.

This is when I pulled a Graycie and went in for the jugular.

"Yep," I said. "They'll sleep in your beds. And you know what? They might even go wee wee in them!"

That was it: enough to trigger fits of hysterical howling in both girls and enough tears to assure that our little unplanned overseas venture was not going to come to pass.

I'm sure to some it's hard to believe that the deal breaker was a small creature that weighs less than a dinner plate. But even though the thought of strangers wetting their beds was the nail in the coffin, our girls truly could not bear to abandon their Graycie bird, any more than they could abandon anything else they'd grown to love and considered part of their home. Had Graycie been pawned off on someone else, would she have fared all right? Well, I've discovered it's done plenty often with pet birds. Parrots live a *long* time. Sometimes life plans change and can no longer incorporate things like exotic pets. But certainly the girls and I weren't prepared to do that to her. Who knows, maybe down the road Scott and I will move overseas and leave Graycie with one of the kids. But for the time being, our house, our things, and most important our pets were safe with us.

CHAPTER 15

A Wish for Santa

Beau passed away during our first year in the new house. We'd given up on her Prozac, which made her so loopy, and instead she was relegated to a lifetime supply of prednisone, which wasn't ideal but actually was preferable to her being stoned and confused all the time.

She loved the new digs and looked forward to walking to the bus stop each day with the kids. One day while walking down the street with the sun shining on her back, we discovered several lumps we hadn't noticed on her before. I took her to the vet, who after biopsying them, thought that one of them seemed suspicious and recommended we have them removed.

Beau, old and grizzled but aside from that seemingly healthy, went in for her routine surgery on a snowy winter day. We were concerned about a ten-year-old dog undergoing an operation, but it seemed to make sense to go through with it. When I picked her up at the end of the day, she staggered to the car, knocking into walls and slipping on the ice and snow outside. I figured the residual anesthesia hadn't worn off yet.

But days, then weeks, later, Beau remained quite disoriented, and soon began wandering off. We kept a good-enough eye on her, and we'd usually catch her before she got very far. She'd never left our yard, not once. She was like a doddering old grandpa—the ones for whom police issue all-points bulletins when they wander off unattended. She also began to lose bladder control at least several times a week. Cleanup duties began extending to Beau's mess, too.

Then one night Beau wandered off and we couldn't find her. We all searched for her until well past bedtime, to no avail. Late that night Scott was at work in his basement office when he heard a faint yelp. It was almost imperceptible, so he went outside to try to home in on where the sound was coming from. Our house backed up to extensive woods, so it was anybody's guess.

At about three in the morning he came into the bedroom and turned on the lights.

"Jen, get up, I need your help," he said.

I dragged myself out of bed, squinting in the harsh light.

"What the hell did you do to yourself?" I asked. He was cut and scratched all over, and blood seeped from several wounds.

"If you think this looks bad, you should see Beau."

I helped Scott deal with his cuts, and then we performed first aid on Beau in the kitchen, washing clean her many scrapes. Scott told me that he had found her entangled in a thicket of sharp bramble bushes, where she would have eventually died had he not heard her cries. We decided it was time to end Beau's suffering.

But by morning, we'd lost the enthusiasm for that plan, as we saw the kids' faces brighten with news of Beau's rescue. They felt so certain that whatever had overtaken her was a temporary condition. But her disorientation worsened rapidly throughout the day, and Scott and I had to make a decision we had desperately avoided.

"It's time, you know," he said to me as we stared into Beau's vacant eyes.

Tears welled up in my own. "She's been there for everything," I said. "I don't know how to let her go. And the kids are going to be devastated."

"But she's suffering, Jen. We can't let this go on and then have her wander off somewhere to die on her own."

I knew this. We both knew this. But Beau had been with us almost from the beginning of our marriage. She'd borne witness to everything we'd gone through as a family. However, Scott was right, it was time.

We kept her comfortable and had many long talks with the kids, and a few days later we reluctantly set up an appointment with our vet to bring Beau in to be put down. The night before, we all spent hours saying teary goodbyes to the dog. I don't think anyone slept a wink that night. At dawn Scott and Kyle decided to take Beau out for one last walk in the woods together. They were gone for an hour when Kyle crashed through the screen door excitedly.

"Mom! Guess what?" he asked, out of breath. "Beau's all better!"

I didn't want to break it to Kyle that Beau wasn't going to get better. But then the dog came into the house, and unbelievably, she was seemingly back to her normal self. She no longer sported that hollow look in her eyes, she recognized her name when we called her, and she inhaled her breakfast, something she hadn't done in weeks.

Scott and I looked at each other.

"We can't do this," he said.

"Nope."

And for a week or so, Beau had returned to us. But then she wandered off again, and her confusion settled in for good.

This was the first time we had to deal with the decline of a beloved pet. On that final morning with her, Beau, ever the trouper, wore a crown of flowers the girls made for her, and we all savored every minute we had with her during those last goodbyes. Before the kids had to leave for school, five-year-old Gillian, our stoic child, went about calming her older brother and sister and assuring them that all would be all right. Graycie, sensing our sadness, chimed in as well, and reassured us, "It's okay!"

Of course nothing's okay when you have to put a family pet down. Even one who had been fairly problematic for a long time.

In the following weeks, while walking to the school bus, Kyle and Kendall held their arms skyward.

"What are you two doing?" I asked the first time they did this.

"Walking Beau up in heaven," they said.

~~~~~

We swore off dogs after Beau's death. Though we missed her, life was much easier with just Graycie and the cats.

One Friday afternoon several months after Beau passed away, Scott's parents came for a visit. As we sat out on the back deck beneath the cool autumn sun, Keith asked us, "So, when are you getting another dog?"

"Never," Scott and I replied in unison.

"You will," Mia said, laughing. "That's what we've said over the years, but it's only a matter of time."

"Not gonna happen," I reaffirmed.

A week later, with the cold weather setting in, we decided we needed to go on a mission to find a fireplace screen. After one of Kyle's soccer games, we all drove north about an hour to a home decor warehouse that had an outdoor sale each fall. When we arrived at the large property situated on a stretch of farmland, we told the kids to stick nearby, as we were only getting a fireplace screen and getting out since Scott's friend Buddy and his family were coming for a visit later that afternoon.

"We've got to get back home to get ready for our guests," Scott said as we pulled in. "So don't go far, and remember: we're just getting a fireplace screen."

Ever the cooperative kids, ours nodded in agreement. Which should've been a red flag.

We parked the car a few feet away from where a cluster of people had gathered, and the kids made a beeline toward the crowd. The attraction turned out to be a group of volunteers from the local animal shelter, who were taking advantage of a stellar fall afternoon to try to unload some of their charges on unwitting customers. The type of people who might be shopping for a fireplace screen.

Kendall spotted the youngest puppy first.

"Look!" she squealed. The other two followed.

"Awww, Mom. Look how cute she is!" Kyle said.

She was indeed cute. Smaller than a cereal bowl, with pointy little ears that bent over toward her face and the deepest blue eyes I'd ever seen on a dog or a human.

Before the kids even contemplated holding her, Scott and

I let them know any attempts to bring the dog home would be futile.

"Look, you can hold that puppy, but that's it. We are not getting another dog. Do you understand?" I asked, looking each child in the eye.

Of course they all nodded their heads, then rushed over to the puppy.

"You kids stay here and we'll be back in ten minutes," Scott said.

We were no sooner at the fireplace screen display than the kids found us and began their full-court press.

Gillian and Kendall went first. "Oh, Mommy, she's the sweetest little puppy! Can't we have her *please?*" Kendall begged.

"No! And if you don't stop lobbying for the dog, you'll have to stand here with us and choose a fireplace screen, and I know you don't want to do that."

The girls reluctantly slunk back toward the puppy, then sent Kyle in their stead. "She's so adorable. And she's really calm. Can't we please have a puppy? Please?"

Scott and I looked at each other, then looked at Kyle.

"*No!*" we barked (no dog pun intended).

We couldn't have been more unequivocal on this point. We were simply not up for raising a puppy. We had two aging cats and Graycie to deal with already, and I really enjoyed not having recently shed fur cascading like tumbleweeds across my hardwood floors each time the furnace blew out air. (Although I will admit I'd noticed a huge uptick in crumbs on the floor after Beau died.)

Scott and I continued to scour the fireplace screens and found nothing even remotely appealing. But not before a couple more visits from the kids, who were nonchalantly putting on the squeeze.

"We'll feed her and walk her," they insisted. "We'll do everything! Really, we will!"

I was going to get a sore neck from shaking my head back and forth with such vehemence.

"What is it about *no* that you're not understanding?"

"Awww, but she's so adorable!"

"Yeah, she's cute. So are you guys, but we're not lining up for another one of you. We cannot take on any more responsibilities right now!"

That was right about when Scott pulled me aside.

"She is awfully cute," he said.

"Cute doesn't feed itself, or pick up the poop in the backyard," I said. "And are you going to wake up with a puppy at three in the morning to take it outside? 'Cause I'm not. Plus, we all agreed that if we ever got another puppy it would be a yellow Lab."

"Well, they say pound dogs make the best pets," he replied. To which I simply rolled my eyes. They schmey.

As soon as we got back to the kids, Kendall, who'd been snuggling with the puppy, thrust her into my arms. For a second I thought, *She's so docile. And with those adorable floppy ears and the sapphire eyes and soft fur, how could we go wrong?* But I quickly shook off my weakness.

"Look, kids, we have to get home," I said. "Say goodbye to the puppy!" I gave the pup a little wave for emphasis and set her down just as a woman and her daughter walked over to check her out.

"Bridget! Look how cute she is!"

My kids and I did a double take. We'd agreed shortly after

Beau died that the next dog we owned, we'd name Bridget. It was a sign.

I zoomed in to wedge myself between the dog and any other takers.

"You swear on a stack of Bibles you'll all help out with this puppy?" I asked, addressing my children like a drill sergeant.

Their heads nodded with earnest vigor.

"And you promise I can have my yellow Lab someday?" I asked Scott.

"I swear it," he said.

I picked up the puppy and held her so we were nose to nose.

"Well, Miss Bridget, looks like today's your lucky day."

～～～～

Turns out the reason Bridget was so docile was the preponderance of parasites and worms that had overtaken her little body. After a couple of rounds of deworming, Bridget would prove to be nearly as high-maintenance as Graycie and far more energetic. Once she was cured, she became a supercharged dynamo with a nasty nipping problem. After a few sessions of puppy kindergarten, we were told by the veterinarian instructor that we needed to get rid of her, immediately.

"She's extremely dominant," the instructor said. "A dog like this could pose a danger to your family and all around her."

By then I had no choice but to be Bridget's staunchest defender.

"But our children love her!" I said. "She's part of our family!"

The vet calculated Bridget's age on her fingers. "I'll tell you what: you've got maybe six weeks left to establish your dominance over this dog. After that, you can forget about it. And don't hold out hope that you'll be able to dominate her enough."

We dominated the living daylights out of Bridget, forbidding any nips with a firm grip on her snout, and poking and prodding every inch of her body to teach her we were her bosses. But as the days progressed, my husband became more convinced that we needed to find a "farm" for Bridget. We all knew what that meant.

"We can't do that! The kids would be devastated. You saw how they handled Beau's death."

Still, Scott contacted the shelter we'd gotten her from and was told that if we didn't keep her, we were contractually bound to hand the dog back over to them. And it wasn't a no-kill shelter. They insisted we were forbidden from finding a new home for her ourselves.

"Scott, she'd be killed! We can't let that happen to her," I said. He agreed.

We decided that if we were to find a new home for the puppy, we wouldn't let the shelter know. Why was it their business if they were going to kill her anyhow? Just as Scott found what appeared to be a "farm" for the dog, with a specious new "owner," we started hearing rumors that there was a stray dog trafficking operation that thrived in our area, because of the medical teaching and research facilities nearby. Supposedly stray dogs were fair game, and people turning in dogs were paid just like they'd be paid to collect recyclable bottles. It might've been merely urban legend, but we didn't want to take the chance.

Soon Christmastime arrived and we still hadn't figured out what to do about Bridget, who was by then about three months old. When seven-year-old Kendall sat in Santa's lap at an annual "breakfast with Santa" we attended with our friends, she had one simple wish.

"Please let Bridget stop being dominant."

Sweet, right? But what was it with us and dominant pets that we couldn't get rid of in good conscience? Bridget was essentially the canine version of Graycie—another wild animal who'd somehow come under our auspices—and we had such guilt-ridden morals we were completely incapable of unloading our untoward pets, or even resisting them in the first place. Scott and I felt awful that Kendall believed a simple request for some Christmas fairy dust could undo what nature had imbued in our pup. Bridget was wild and determined for a reason: she was a survivor, just like Graycie. Had either of them been more submissive, they'd likely have not lived long enough to become part of our family.

Christmas morning arrived cold and gray. Kyle and Gillian raced downstairs to open their presents; Kendall's attention was focused solely on Bridget, who lay on the floor, calm and quiet, not once biting or nipping or growling or acting like the wild puppy she'd been the day before. Not all day, not all week, not for several weeks. The smile on Kendall's face that day was as wide as the ocean, so thrilled was she with the power of her special Christmas wish. I don't think she left her beloved pup's side until bedtime.

Eventually, we returned to puppy classes, whereupon the vet pulled us aside at the end of class yet again.

"I must say I didn't think this dog would improve," she said. "I'm downright shocked, but you've managed to dominate her."

In the weeks to come we learned that Bridget had switched

her dominance of humans to a dominance of dogs, which over the years has been a real pain in the butt. And she has reasserted her dominance over us at certain times, when stressed or tired or jealous or sick, but she's always been manageable enough.

As with all of our pets, Bridget taught us some valuable lessons. In particular, she proved to us that Christmas miracles can indeed happen, and also that, as Scott said, pound pups can make the best pets. If only we could assert our dominance over Graycie the way we managed to over Bridget, we'd have been in fine shape.

CHAPTER 16

Jungle Love and the Girl from Ipanema

Kendall and I continued to enjoy taking Bridget to puppy classes; she'd especially bonded with the pooch and spent lots of free time working on behavioral tricks we learned. The kids, who by then were almost ten, eight, and six, were getting older and becoming more entrenched in our neighborhood and more involved with the care and maintenance of our pets, and all in all life was going wonderfully. We'd even started holding Graycie on our hands again at night while watching television—a real milestone for our fickle parrot. During this time—before the kids were involved in travel sports and other time-consuming activities—we spent a lot of time at home. The kids in the neighborhood liked to gather in our large backyard to play regular games of capture the flag and flashlight tag, and on many evenings before dinner, neighbors stopped by to share a friendly glass of wine and catch up.

It was interesting to see how much more receptive Graycie was toward such visitors than toward us. We'd discovered this early on to some degree—whenever Buddy came to our house, Graycie acted like a young girl whose heart-throb crush had just shown up to court her. Buddy is one of those guys who puts people at ease the minute they're in his presence—a real people person. However, he must also be a parrot person. Every time he's encountered Graycie—and sometimes it's been years in between visits—he goes right up to her, speaks in a soothing voice, and begins to pet her from head to tail, and Graycie just cocks her head toward him to encourage more petting, loving the attention.

Scott and I merely shake our heads, considering that if we attempted the same maneuver she'd more than likely bite our fingers off. I can't explain it. Buddy has the slightest hint of a drawl to his voice, and sometimes I wonder if it's the suggestion of an accent that appeals to Graycie—she definitely has an affinity for foreigners—but as everyone knows, sometimes matters of the heart defy explanation.

While Buddy holds a special place in Graycie's heart, the most beloved object of her affection to date was our neighbor Carolina. Carolina was a complete hottie, a Charo-like Brazilian who lived across the street from us for a couple of years. The first time Carolina came over and saw Graycie, she started cooing in her coochie-coochie sex-charged Brazilian accent, and Graycie had a friend for life. The more we got to know Carolina, the more demonstrative she became with Graycie, and she would prance over in her clingy little outfits, trailing a cloud of provocative perfume, sometimes with a flute of champagne in her hand. She'd shimmy and shake for the bird and stroke her feathers, and life could not have gotten much finer for that parrot. She was like a bored husband who ignores his wife but beams with effervescence when greeting the new nubile receptionist at work each morning.

It was at that time—when Graycie was about ten years old—that we became convinced she was really a boy. I mean, Carolina had entered Graycie's life and my bird was beyond smitten, whistling catcalls, practically lurching at our neighbor, dipping her head for pets and hoisting her red feathers for Carolina to stroke. I sort of felt like the parent whose child preferred the babysitter after a while, but then again everyone preferred Carolina if given the choice: How could you not love a sexy Latin lady with long, shiny brown hair, a booty that launched vivid male imaginations, and an air of confidence born of regular success with such tools?

Graycie's next love was Anne Marie, who, interestingly enough, moved into Carolina's home when her family moved. Anne Marie hailed from New Zealand and had that very practical Dr. Doolittle know-how with animals that seems to cause all sorts of beasts to fall in line accordingly. She was about the only person who could force our crazed dingo dog, Bridget, into submission with just one word. Maybe growing up on a ranch with a lot of sheep made her into some sort of animal whisperer, but her no-nonsense approach to my parrot worked wonders.

Anne Marie needed to only show up and head straight to the cage, and Graycie was all ears, perked up and ready to receive her visitor like a queen. She offered up her head for scratches, and sometimes even her chin, which Graycie has never offered up to me. She was a tramp for the cause! At this point I gave up being jealous—whatever I lacked was what they had, and I couldn't just cook it up out of nowhere. Besides, I was happy that Grayce was getting what she needed from someone, even if it wasn't me.

Then there was Michael, yet another accented object of Graycie's lust. Michael was a neighborhood friend of ours, a British lord who was living in the States for a while. When he and his wife, Nancy, would come to our house for dinner, Michael would divert his way over to the bird and stand petting her for fifteen, twenty minutes nonstop with nary a nip. Never in my life have I gotten in more than maybe thirty seconds of petting without retaliation (and that was easily fifteen years ago). I could never compete with his refined British accent, so I've just accepted the fact that I'll never win Graycie's heart in quite the same ways. Graycie's flirtations with Michael led us to wonder yet again whether Graycie was a boy or a girl. We had been so convinced of her male status after her shameless behavior with Carolina, but now she seemed to have eyes only for Michael. The question of her gender would later be revealed with shocking clarity.

I take solace in the fact that other than charming foreigners, the sound that truly inspires Graycie is the sound of 3M packing tape. Because Scott's office is in our basement, on many days he'll prepare boxes to be shipped out. Whenever that big 3M tape dispenser comes out, with the loud ripping sound that accompanies the pull of tape to package, Graycie goes into paroxysms of jungle screeching. She then repeats the tape-ripping sound over and over. It makes me a little bit sad when she does it, because sometimes I wonder if she thinks the sound is coming from that elusive mate she's been searching for all these years. As Graycie has made me painfully aware, waiting for a creature to return your affection can be a frustrating experience.

CHAPTER 17

Pizza! Pizza!

Call me a cynic, but when things are going too well, I feel like there's always something lurking around the corner. And on an otherwise glorious May evening, we turned that corner.

"The EEG indicates that your daughter is continuing to experience little seizures," the doctor informed us, choking back her tears. As I tried to digest this information, the part about "little seizures," all I could picture was a cartoonish bald midget in a toga, jumping up and down, squawking "Pizza! Pizza!"—I was having flashbacks to the Little Caesars pizza commercial. Little Caesars, little seizures.

Unable to process the gravity of the situation, I could only focus on the absurd. How we found ourselves in the pediatric unit at a major medical center that evening—just a few days after my daughter had experienced her first grand mal seizure—being told that our child had a serious neurological condition was beyond my comprehension. I didn't know then that what lay before us would be an experience that would leave its stain on my mind for years to come.

The saga had begun a few days earlier. We'd barely tucked the kids into bed for the night when I heard a gagging, choking noise. Racing toward the source, I found eight-year-old Kendall in bed, eyes rolled back in her head, her whole body in spasms.

"Scott, quick, come here!" I shouted.

Kyle arrived first, and started screaming for his father to hurry up. My husband, whose college friend had seizures, immediately recognized what was occurring.

"Call 9-1-1," Scott said calmly. He sat with Kendall as she was flailing and jerking while my trembling fingers sought out the suddenly impossibly small buttons on the phone. How could he remain calm while our daughter gasped for breath?

While we waited the interminable fifteen minutes until emergency help arrived, I called the only doctor I knew—a friend's husband—thinking as long as we had a doctor nearby, maybe Kendall wouldn't die. I hadn't considered how much a urologist would know about seizures. In the dark days ahead, I was able to laugh about how, while we actually needed a *neurologist,* at least our friend's medical specialty rhymed. When the seizure finally subsided after several minutes, Kendall lay motionless for about half an hour, staring aimlessly. Our doctor friend explained to us this was the postictal phase that occurs after a large seizure. Her body and brain had performed the equivalent of a marathon, he said, and both were exhausted. All we knew was, she exhibited no speech skills, no response, no sign of recognition. The lively, spirited child we'd put to bed half an hour ago was nowhere to be found. In her place lay a near lifeless zombie, which was how the EMTs found her when they arrived.

The following hour was a blur. EMTs, walkie-talkies

squawking, crowded Kendall's room, testing her responses and vital statistics, calling results in to their transmitters, making sure she was stabilized. She was then loaded into an ambulance, by then more lucid but still totally uncommunicative.

The irony did not escape me that Gillian, who would wake at the brush of a leaf on her window, slept through a parade of boots stomping up and down the steps, walkie-talkies and the parrot squawking back and forth at each other (Graycie was issuing her jungle call that would easily alert a fellow African gray a mile away that something was amiss), and the dog barking an insane chorus of alarms. Our neighbor stayed with Kyle and Gillian while we went to the hospital; Scott, the more clearheaded of the two of us, went with Kendall in the ambulance, and I followed in my car.

We spent about four hours in the ER as the doctors ran through clinical tests of Kendall's neurological responses. As she'd had no head injury, illness, or family history of seizures, the ER doctor determined that Kendall's seizure was idiopathic, meaning there was no known cause. Because her vital statistics looked good, her responses were returning, and she was able to talk, he sent us home, suggesting we get some sleep and see our pediatrician in the morning.

But to us Kendall still seemed pretty out of it. She was talking as if there was a frosted glass wall between her and us, and she seemed fuzzy, confused, disoriented. While aware of her surroundings, she said her thinking seemed muddled and foggy. It reminded me of when Beau came out of her surgically induced anesthesia.

We saw the pediatrician first thing the next morning. The by-now-familiar neurological exam we'd seen performed repeatedly in the ER just hours earlier began anew: he had Kendall touch her nose with her fingers, touch her fingers with arms extended, walk a straight line, and extend her arms, palms to the ceiling, and hold. My daughter's once-steady hands trembled. Kendall remained cheerful but complained that her head felt strange—as if memories were swirling rapidly through her brain—and spoke in an uncharacteristically soft and tentative voice.

Nevertheless, the pediatrician determined that Kendall was doing well. "Sometimes these things just happen," he told us. "Hopefully we won't have any more problems. We'll schedule a series of tests—an MRI, EEG, CT scan—sometime in the next several weeks just to rule things out. Until then, just go on about your lives normally."

On the way home, we stopped for lunch at a nearby restaurant, where Kendall ordered fries. As she was reaching for her drink, her arm dropped onto her plate into a pool of ketchup.

"What just happened?" I asked, panicked.

"I don't know, it just fell," she said.

Moments later, while lifting her glass, her arm again fell, spilling water everywhere. Immediately we phoned the pediatrician, who ordered us to the hospital.

Over the next three days, Scott and I took turns at the hospital while the other shuttled Kyle and Gillian to and from school, made their meals, fed the pets, and showered when possible. The kids were amazingly helpful while we remained in this limbo, doing whatever we asked of them without complaint. The pets? Well, they had to deal with getting fed sporadically and not having the freedom to go outside— or play outside the cage—they were used to, but what could we do?

The CT scan and MRI eliminated some of the worst-case

scenarios, such as brain tumors or strokes, thank god. Yet we were still in the dark.

It was a gorgeous Friday afternoon when we learned the diagnosis. The pediatric neurologist on call said the EEG indicated that Kendall had childhood seizure disorder, which fell under the rubric of the neurological disorder epilepsy. She said Kendall would need to take medication for at least two years to try to stop the seizure activity, and Kendall's blood levels would need to be checked regularly for liver toxicity and potential bone marrow suppression that could occur from the meds.

Scott and I were stunned.

"What about all the bad things that might occur from these medicines?" I asked Scott, as if he had any more answers than I did.

"We don't have a choice in the matter. We're just going to have to go ahead with them and see what happens," he said. I tend to be the more alarmist of the two of us, and I was happy to lean on his certainty that things would work out. However, I had nagging doubts.

"But there are all of these things related to the medication that could hurt her. Which is worse? The seizures, a damaged liver, or who knows what else?"

We had no answers, and had to plug on with whatever information we could garner. So we returned home with a fragile child, a prescription for a potentially toxic new medicine, and a fear of allowing Kendall to do many things that kids take for granted: swimming, climbing trees, ice skating. What if Kendall had a seizure while biking, and got hit by a car? Or while swimming, and drowned? Until her medicine worked effectively—an indefinite period of time that could be weeks or months—the doctor said she should avoid all these activities unless continually supervised. Kendall would live a caged life alongside Graycie.

During those first few weeks it seemed to us that Kendall had suffered some loss from this seizure. Her cognitive skills were lagging; her handwriting was reduced to kindergarten scrawl, and simple mathematical equations were a struggle. She'd only recently scored in the ninety-eighth percentile in cognitive ability tests at school, yet she could no longer print her name legibly. Her hands trembled, unable to readily pick up small things such as M&M's. Was this temporary or permanent? We didn't know quite how long her seizure had lasted. Could it have caused loss of oxygen to the brain?

Theories differ on whether a seizure adversely affects a brain. Some experts think not at all. Others compare it to a boxer's being hit repeatedly in the head: the longer and more intense the seizure, the more trauma to the brain. My simple logic tended to put me in the latter camp. What I was seeing in Kendall bolstered my fears. I worried that we would have to relearn Kendall, and that she would have to relearn everything. I found myself grieving for unexpected things. Kendall, always fascinated with space exploration, could never become an astronaut—only those with impeccable health records qualify for that job. I dreaded the day I'd have to break that news to her.

When Kendall was released from the hospital, we were given information on ramping up the medicine, Tegretol, and the pager number of the neurology resident who treated her in the hospital. While we were assigned a neurologist, all questions were vetted through the resident. It became my full-time job to learn simple neurology (an oxymoron). And I soon found that while I needed a veritable medical degree to understand it, I needed an even greater degree of patience to deal with neurologists.

Immediately we put out feelers to determine the best doctor available to treat our daughter, and we settled on Dr. Johnson, an esteemed expert in the field of pediatric neurology. During this crucial first month, Kendall never had a day during which she felt well, let alone normal. She often said her brain felt strange, but struggled to convey what she was experiencing, and she frequently had to stop activities until these feelings subsided. Unable to resume school yet, she felt isolated. Desperate to heal our daughter, we assumed our alliance with Dr. Johnson would help achieve this goal, but he proved to be inaccessible. After our initial brief visit with him, during which he insisted that Kendall continue taking the meds that she needed—despite my voicing my fears that they might be doing more damage than good—we were on our own. We could reach him only through the neurology resident. We'd contact her, who would contact him, who might then contact us . . . a twisted perversion of the childhood game of telephone.

In the meantime, Kendall's condition deteriorated. As the weeks progressed, she became more tentative in her actions, quiet, and withdrawn. She experienced "drop seizures," in which some body part—neck, arm, leg—would suddenly and arbitrarily lose support, sort of like those little tchotchke toys where you push a button at the bottom and the little person collapses. She would often have a glazed, disoriented look in her eyes.

I suspected that the drug prescribed to Kendall to reduce seizure activity was actually enhancing it; it seemed that as we gradually increased her dosage, as per the doctor's orders, the drop seizures increased in frequency. After Kendall fell down a flight of steps for the third time in one week, I demanded a call back from Dr. Johnson.

"Mrs. Gardiner," he began, his arrogant tone barely disguising his disdain for a mere unenlightened mother, "this medicine is helping her. She needs it. You must be patient. These things take time."

Time was not an option when our child could no longer reliably negotiate a flight of steps, or lift a mug full of hot soup to her mouth, without fear of injury. We needed to seek counsel elsewhere.

Nearly two months after our ordeal began, we drove several hours away to meet with Dr. Chandler, a renowned pediatric neurologist whose work we'd read about, and who determined that Kendall's seizures were negligible.

"Had you brought her here first, we probably wouldn't have put her on any medicine," he told us after his examination.

The doctor, unconcerned with the changes we'd noticed in Kendall's demeanor, did not feel that the seizure activity shown on Kendall's EEG merited the use of anticonvulsants. He noted that she seemed lovely to him, and that was that.

We were learning there were many schools of thought on seizures, but we didn't know in which school to enroll. We now had the advice of two seasoned neurologists with divergent opinions, neither with an explanation for our daughter's ongoing malaise. We also got no consensus on what kind of seizures Kendall was experiencing. Her EEG was not definitive, leading to subjective interpretation. Were they benign rolandic, typical of childhood seizures and imminently out-

growable? Or temporal lobe, which could potentially mani-
fest in more unstable emotional behavior? Would Kendall's
seizures increase in frequency and intensity, so that she would
end up wearing a helmet to protect her skull from potentially
dangerous seizure-related falls? Should we attempt to put her
on an extremely rigid and not widely approved high-fat keto-
genic diet, which is touted by some as a radical means to completely end, or at least drastically reduce, seizure problems in
extreme cases?

By now it was summertime—swimming season. Reluctant
to allow Kendall, a passionate swimmer, into the pool without
constant supervision, we compromised and decided—to her
great dismay—to have her wear a bright pink swim cap so that
I could easily watch her. We'd finally persuaded the diffident
Dr. Johnson to switch to a different seizure medication after
Kendall fell off her bike as a result of a seizure of some kind.
Depakote, the next drug of choice, didn't do much better for
her. Her once-effervescent spirit seemed dulled by the effects,
her personality became bland, and she became sluggish, albeit
in a different way than the first medicine had rendered her.

Scott and I knew we needed some answers. An SOS to a
large online quilting group to which I belonged yielded rec-
ommendations for a pediatric neurologist only two hours
away from us in the D.C. area. After our limited experience,
Dr. Golden would prove to be a rarity in the world of neurology we'd experienced so far: he was warm and courteous,
willing to listen, flexible in considering treatment options,
friendly, and giving of his time. He had a quality vital to any
good doctor: empathy. For the first time since our journey began, we knew we had an ally in our neurologist.

"I know that many neurologists won't even think about

taking a kid off the meds for at least two years," he said. "But in light of the opinion of Dr. Chandler, and after reading Kendall's EEG report, I'm perfectly comfortable with trying to wean her off."

As EEGs are subject to varying interpretations, he at least was willing to work through trial and error to determine for certain the right course of treatment for our daughter: whether she actually needed the medicine or we could completely take her off it.

Kendall began the next school year as she was weaning off the Depakote, which she finished in late September. I received daily calls from school reporting that Kendall was feeling strange and struggling in class, and many days I'd no sooner drop her at school then have to bring her back home. In October, I got the call I'd been dreading.

"You need to come in right away, something's terribly wrong with Kendall," the school receptionist said. The teacher said Kendall had been sitting in class, staring at the board. Finally, she stood up and said, "Who are you? I don't know where I am. I need my mom."

By the time I got there, she was only slightly more aware of her surroundings. I called Dr. Golden's pager from the car; he told us to bring her to the office first thing in the morning for an EEG. The next day, the doctor was called into the room midway through Kendall's test.

"Yeah, just what I thought." Dr. Golden frowned, pointing at the screen. "Look at this reading—this side of her brain is flatlining." In layman's terms, part of her brain just wasn't working; it had temporarily shut down. A big seizure had happened, maybe not as intense as the first one, but it was not a good sign. Disappointed, we put Kendall back on Depakote.

Seizure drugs often have to be tweaked to achieve correct dosage levels, and we now had to actually increase the dose from her previous amount. We were sorely unprepared for the radical effect this would have on Kendall's brain.

By the time her meds were at the prescribed dosage level a few weeks later, our child was a virtual stranger, prone to extremes in temperament and completely unable to function academically. One minute she'd happily play with her siblings, the next she'd shriek at them. Occasionally, she'd sit on the ground rocking back and forth catatonically, and once I found her thrashing about on all fours, screeching at the top of her lungs like an animal. Sometimes I would retreat to my room and sob. How could I have put a child to bed so innocently one night, and never know that person again? Meanwhile, Ken's problems were affecting Kyle and Gillian. Most nights Gillian woke repeatedly with nightmares; Scott and I, already emotionally drained, became physically exhausted. The kids, echoing our stress and tension, bickered constantly. And the menagerie of pets? Who could deal with them? It was about that time that Graycie took to asking frequently, "Whatsamatter?" Parroting me, words I asked Kendall constantly.

I called Dr. Golden, and again expressed my concern about Kendall's behavior. He suggested we switch her to Lamictal, a newer yet very expensive drug, one he'd seen promising results from. Kendall was to start this gradually while weaning off the Depakote, so there would be an overlap of two drugs for a while.

A few weeks into the weaning process, Kendall joined Scott on a five-day business trip to Manhattan. Each year he took one of the kids on a business trip with him, an annual tradition they enjoyed with their dad. While he worked the trade show, Kendall played at the on-site child care. Meanwhile, Kyle, Gillian, and I stayed home and enjoyed a few days' respite. When they returned, I was shocked to see Kendall's ghastly gray pallor and observe her sluggishness.

As soon as I got Scott alone, I grilled him. "What's up with Kendall?"

"What do you mean?"

"Can't you tell how sickly she looks? She looks like death warmed over!"

"Honestly, I didn't notice any difference."

The transformation in her had occurred so gradually over the week of their trip it hadn't been obvious to Scott.

I immediately called Dr. Golden's office. As always, I had to leave a voice message; calls were triaged and sometimes took weeks before they were returned. Days later, I was still waiting for a response. Then a nurse friend mentioned that she thought Kendall looked quite sick. I called the neurologist's office yet again. "I want a goddamned call back and I want it now," I screamed into the receiver. "Something is wrong with my child, and I am not going to wait until she is dead to find out why you people don't have the decency to return an urgent phone call."

Now, I can appreciate how frenzied a neurologist's office can be. Spending just a short time in the waiting room of one has reinforced in my mind, "But for the grace of God go I." Most people who see neurologists have really bad problems. And as agonizing as our daughter's condition was to us, and as much as it unsettled our lives and adversely affected us all enormously, our situation was nothing compared to that of most of the other patients under these doctors' care. Usually

I understood why our calls rarely got returned in good time. But not this time. My ranting yielded immediate results, and Dr. Golden agreed to see Kendall the next day.

First he administered a brief test to determine Kendall's reading comprehension. When he was done, he said, "See, she's perfectly normal, she's working at an age-appropriate lower third-grade level."

"Yes, but nine months ago, she was at a seventh-grade level," I replied. Dr. Golden decided to accelerate the weaning off Depakote, and finally we started to see the old Kendall return. Her coloring, her wacky sense of humor . . . she even started dancing around the house and teasing her siblings again. She could print legibly, and she didn't have to concentrate so intensely before speaking, as if whatever was in her brain was stuck and unable to exit through her mouth.

A few months later, I took her back to see Dr. Golden. "Wow, she seems so much better now," he said, beaming.

"Yeah, we can't believe that we finally got our Kendall back," I said, smiling. "That Depakote really messed her up."

"Oh, yeah, well, I told you about Depakote dementia." He laughed.

Well, no, he didn't, actually. But when I went home, I went online and researched it to find out what he meant. I was floored at my findings. Buried amid reams of pharmacological information about this medicine, in very fine print, under "Adverse Reactions," it read: "Other Patient Populations, Psychiatric: Emotional upset, depression, psychosis, aggression, hyperactivity, hostility, and behavioral deterioration." Everything I had pointed out to the experts for months and months, but they had shrugged off. And here it was, in black and white.

My daughter may have lost a year of her life because no one was reading the fine print.

While it took a long time for us to find a medicine that worked for Kendall, it's important to note that those other drugs do work for plenty of people with seizures. They just were the wrong drugs for our child. Kendall remained trouble-free on Lamictal for several years, until we decided to attempt to wean her off the medicine when she was thirteen.

We were anxious to get Kendall off medication altogether; the long-term effects of it on her body are unknown. But after so many years of turmoil for our family, we didn't want to leap too suddenly and live to regret it, so we consulted the doctor and carefully laid out a plan. After about six months of weaning, we toasted Ken's final dose with water in champagne glasses.

Our elation was short-lived. Three days later, just minutes before leaving on a class ski trip, Kendall blacked out. It was fleeting, lasting only thirty seconds. We fought to get an EEG on our daughter the next day. The following week, the doctor told us Ken's EEG appeared normal. "Well then what exactly happened to Kendall last week?" I probed.

He pored through the complicated data in front of him, comparing it with previous EEGs, and noticed a subtle change that appeared consistent with her previous tests.

"You know what? This does indicate some seizure activity, and it was good that you insisted on having this test performed immediately," he said. "If we'd waited till today, this would never have shown up."

Feeling slightly vindicated for our persistence, we were nevertheless disappointed at the result, and reluctantly restarted her meds. We were truly fortunate that Kendall didn't have the seizure while suspended in midair on a ski lift, which could have been deadly.

Finally, about a year later, Kendall was able to successfully wean off her seizure medicine. We will forever hope this is something that remains in our past, an experience that defined us all in many ways, but helped us to grow stronger as individuals, and as a family.

CHAPTER 18

Puppies, Cage Rage, and Five Minutes' Peace

Okay, so we had a bit of a bump in the road with Kendall's medical situation. But what is life but bumps in the road, and how one chooses to navigate them? We certainly weren't going to be defined by the struggles.

As we climbed out of that little implosion, things continued to improve. The kids were getting older, busier, with sports and musical endeavors and all sorts of things that kept us occupied and engaged in their increasingly hectic lives. And Scott and I were getting older. In fact, for my fortieth birthday, Scott fulfilled his promise about that yellow Labrador in our future, even though he loathed the idea of having two dogs in the house.

I grew up with a host of black Labradors, and they never seemed to be much work. Perhaps that's because I wasn't the one caring for and cleaning up after them. So when I turned forty, we plunked down a huge chunk of money for a Labrador that was virtually assured of not having the myriad issues with which poor old Beau was plagued. We brought home a darling little polar bear of a puppy, a white dumpling with such enormous paws we dubbed her Sasquatch, Sassy for short.

With the addition of Sassy, we finally had a relatively low-maintenance household pet. After all those years, we hit the jackpot. And like with anything that is hard-won, we appreciated her easy existence all the more, having been through so many situations with various creatures along the way.

But in true Gardiner tradition, we couldn't quite leave well enough alone.

Two years after Sassy came along, we decided that she was such an awesome dog, maybe it was a good time to venture into the world of puppies. I know, I know, our last breeding attempt failed miserably, but this one would be scientifically sound. Plus, when I was a kid my family had two litters of puppies and I recalled this experience with such fondness. Scott's family had also bred a couple of litters of puppies when he was a child, and we thought the kids would forever remember how much fun it was to care for a bunch of adorable pups.

And so after going through major effort to get the proper clearance to breed Sassy, ensuring that her hips, teeth, eyes, and overall genetic makeup was of high enough quality to justify reproduction, we put the process in motion by sending her off to a stud farm (which in hindsight seems awfully heartless).

A few months later we ended up with four precious puppies: two yellow Labs, two black ones. And more work than ten people would want to take on. Whatever we were thinking by undertaking this project, I don't know, but I do know now that rearing a litter of young pups involves unbelievable amounts of energy. As much as we loved those four puppies, and as much as it pained us to send them off with new owners when their time was up, we couldn't wait to be free of the heavy responsibility. However, we would always have a reminder: Graycie picked up the shrill yelp the puppies made and occasionally repeats it still—our little memento of the days when we had four sweet little four-legged babies shredding every item within eyeshot to smithereens.

～～～

At about that time, when I would tiptoe downstairs early in the morning to slip out to the gym, I discovered something funny about our parrot. Every day, as I descended the steps in the predawn darkness, from beneath the tattered confines of the sheet that covers her cage at night and saves us from round-the-clock noise pollution, in a low, menacing growl, Graycie would mutter in a voice reminiscent of an angry demon, "What?"

At first, at that early hour, I wondered exactly what she meant. But most often, I laughed. Which isn't such a bad way to start the day, is it?

Perhaps a more appropriate word for Graycie to utter would be "why." As in, "Why the hell would you take care of me for approaching two decades when all I want is your blood?" And sometimes I wonder that myself. But at five-thirty in the morning, that's too deep a thought to actually work through, even for me.

By this point, Graycie was on the cusp of teenager-dom, and with that came obstinate teen behavior and plenty more boundary pushing. As if we didn't have enough of that with our children, we also got to figure out how to negotiate such behavior with an irrational parrot. But whereas the kids would tend to retreat to the solace of their rooms to escape their parents, Graycie simply amplified her demands on us, and her noise level as well.

I'd recently started freelance writing, and therefore had become increasingly aware of how very loud my world was, and how much I needed to get a break from the noise in order to concentrate. I'd long been a writer of sorts; I could knock out a wicked grocery list or Christmas newsletter, no problem. My background was in journalism, and I'd worked in print, radio, and television before I was married, so the process came pretty naturally to me, and my new career kind of fell into my lap. Actually, into a bucket, while I was taking a shower.

Central Virginia had been suffering from a terrible drought, and severe water restrictions had been enacted. One day, as I showered with buckets of water beneath me to catch as much residual water as possible so that I could recycle it for toilet flushing, I started thinking about how greatly the drought was impacting what one would consider very basic things.

For instance, the upcoming holiday season would surely preclude any parties: no one could host a houseful of guests, ply them with drinks all night, yet not allow them to use the facilities. Since our water usage had been halved, no one had spare water to flush. Such a "tragedy" was unthinkable, so I wrote a humorous piece about it and quickly sold it to a local newspaper. My freelance career had been launched, with a deceptively quick sale. Soon after, I was selling my writing to various regional and national publications—though not always with such ease—and recording radio essays for a regional NPR affiliate, and then I landed a column in our daily newspaper. Along the way I decided to try my hand at writing fiction as well.

It was an easy fit for a stay-at-home mom to work as a writer, since my schedule could be worked around my kids'. And as they were in school full-time, I had the house all to myself in which to write in peace.

Except for those darned pets.

One of my favorite children's books we read with our kids until tattered is *Five Minutes' Peace,* which is about an elephant mom who can't find solitude to save her soul. As a mother, I could relate. As a pet owner, even more so. And as a writer, I began to recognize solitude as an underrated commodity that tends to remain just past the horizon.

In the midst of puppies and teens and crazy parrots, I had been working under a self-imposed deadline, with the plans to submit my novel to agents to try to then sell it to a New York publishing house. But with my kids home all summer, I had put off most everything writing-related for as long as I could without feeling like an irresponsible slacker. There was, however, a light at the end of the tunnel: back-to-school time. I decided the first day back for my kids would be the day I would finally reclaim my schedule and behave like the disciplined writer I aspired to be.

The day after Labor Day arrived. I drove my kids to school, then returned home without stopping for cappuccino or pastries or groceries or even gas (I'm a very industrious procrastinator). I shunned the chest-high stockpile of dirty laundry awaiting me in the basement, and instead settled my butt down at my desk, intent on knocking out at least an entire book by noon.

My first distraction came from Bridget, who barks at the mere suggestion of movement within a hundred-yard radius. This can include a leaf blowing outside the window. You can imagine how many leaves blow outside the window of a house that backs up to the woods. Bridget's shrill bark set my teeth on edge, and immediately my ears pinned back like a collie's hearing one of those canine whistles. I tried hard to ignore it.

After about fifteen minutes of intermittent barking, I got up, put her out (with Sassy following obligingly), and again sat down, fingers to the keyboard, ready for my imminent brainstorm. Soon Bridget barked to be let back in. Up again, let them in, back down, ready to get to work. Ah, but everyone wanted a piece of me, so next, the bird got into the act.

Of course Graycie loves to be the center of attention, which is handy since she resides at that unavoidable juncture between our living and dining rooms, overlooking the kitchen. I was not inclined to open the perch up on the cage, because she'd been getting into a lot of mischief, which would only require yet more of my attention. However, Graycie had gotten wise to my disinclination and had figured out a way to let me know in no uncertain terms that SHE WANTS OUT! by plinking on the metal bars with her beak, *plink! plink! plink!* The bird's got staying power, and can plink without cessation for a half an hour easily. You've heard of road rage? Maybe even 'roid rage? Well, Graycie, it seems, had developed a bad case of cage rage.

My intent was not to imprison Graycie, but once her bad-tempered behavior begins, I cannot reward it by caving to her demands. When I can keep an eye on her, I will open the cage, but because she'd recently become so devious (including sneaking off the cage to make mincemeat of my furniture), I knew I couldn't deal with the consequences at that particular time. But after twenty solid minutes of *plink, plank, plink, plank, bing, bang, bong,* I couldn't take it any longer and relented, hating myself all the more for engaging in head games with a parrot.

I approached the bird and stooped to remove the top layer of newspaper from the bottom of the cage—the one littered with wasted parrot chow and dropped food and dropped, um, droppings. As I leaned over, Graycie scurried down the inside of the cage, ever on the prowl for an attack strategy (something she of course does with relish). Reaching through the cage, she was able to grab a chunk of my hair and pull. I looked up to see a shred of blond highlights clamped in her beak.

Helpless, I warned her to behave, and then raced back to the top of the cage to open the perch before she again rushed after me, hoping to maul me before I could safely move away. It was like a game of dodgeball, only I was avoiding a blade instead of a hard leather ball. My parrot has such a charming disposition. Safely out of harm's way, I returned to my computer, ready to get to work.

Immediately Graycie scooted along the bars, beak to claw, beak to claw, to the bottom of the cage, this time on the outside. She'd decided it was time to pull the newspaper sheets out from the bottom of the tray and shred them all over my clean floor. Within ten minutes, enough paper was strewn about to accommodate a nest of large rodents. She'd done this after depositing an enormous splat of bird poo below, which helped to adhere the paper to the hardwood floor. This is why I'd preempted an even larger mess by removing that top sheet beforehand—it's bad enough to have shredded yet somewhat clean newspaper decorating one's living space, but add to it strewn old bits of sticky fruit, decomposing vegetables, and dried bird excrement . . . Martha Stewart would not be impressed.

Rather than allowing myself to be diverted yet again, I decided to ignore the mess and return to my computer. Twenty-plus minutes into my new work regimen, a noticeable silence settled in. I glanced toward the cage, only to realize no bird was either in it or on it. A look under the dining room table revealed Graycie *click-clack*ing her pigeon-toed black talons across the expanse of my dining room, a trail of droppings in her wake and her defiant red tail feathers dragging behind her as if to say "Up yours!" There's something somewhat demeaning about being flipped off by a household pet.

I heaved a sigh and headed over toward the bird. First I suggested to Graycie that she get back onto the cage before the dogs ate her. She looked at me with two words in her eyes: "Yeah, right." She continued wandering astray, with no intention of following my gentle hints.

I've often found that so much in life is based on certain social contracts' working as planned. You take it for granted, for example, that, generally speaking, your kids will obey you. When they become old enough and defiant enough, the jig's up. They've figured out that ultimately, you hold very little sway over them. By then you hope they're conditioned to behave within acceptable social parameters. And so it goes with Graycie, who clearly has realized that she holds the upper hand over me. Only she hasn't picked up on that whole social contract thing yet. And she's got a tool in her arsenal that I am lacking: her menacing, hooked, and ever-so-sharp black keratin beak, a lethal tool for which I have enormous respect. And fear. And loathing. With it she can readily crush the rock-hard shell of a brazil nut. Deforest a home's worth of decorative houseplants. Shred my living room furniture. Or choose to bite my finger off. Maim me. De-eyeball me if she really wanted to. She's not afraid to wield it against me (I have the scars, both physical and mental, to prove it).

So instead of forcing the issue, I retrieved a broom, hoping to scare her back up onto the cage. As I began to sweep, she aggressively chased both me and the broom, biting the bristles and pecking at my ankles, while repeating over and over again "Hello, gray chicken. Hello, gray chicken" in my voice (it's a term of endearment I often call her).

By this time I was entertaining visions of parrot-on-a-spit and was threatening her with parroticide (if that's not a word, it should be). The stubborn bird would simply not comply. To the rescue came Bridget, who had gotten wind of the psittacine escapee on the loose. She careened into the room, nearly toppling the bird. Graycie began flapping her wings, scattering hundreds of bits of newspaper throughout the living room, dining room, and kitchen (curse that open floor plan!), the remnants of a ticker tape parade celebrating her escape. As the dog skidded into the cage, Graycie yelled, "Bridget! NOOOO! You're a BAD, BAD GIRL! Stop it NOW!"

Luckily for her, my murderous notions of throttling her and stuffing her into my electric smoker were replaced by my laughter. But just barely.

At that point, I gave up on bothering with both Graycie and her chaos, and instead took my laptop onto the front porch, where the mess and the pets would remain out of sight, out of mind, and blessedly out of earshot.

CHAPTER 19

Wonderwall and Our Daily Grayce

It's such a true cliché that time gets ahead of you. Somehow one day I was a fresh-faced naïf tentatively grasping a newborn in my arms, terrified I hadn't a clue what to do with him. Flash forward sixteen impossibly fast years, and I was a seasoned veteran who'd practically seen it all with my kids. *Practically.*

Having made it through fall and winter, I found myself once again preoccupied with the usual springtime parental hazing events—I think all parents rue the blitz that is the month of May, in which kids and parents are bombarded with year-end obligations for every sport, activity, academic obligation, and extracurricular activity imaginable. Throw in a handful of field trips that ought to have happened in the dead of winter, a smattering of teacher appreciation meals, and the requisite parties and awards banquets that accompany all of this, and if they're anything like me, parents are surviving in cope mode, checking off the list to get to the next event.

To add to my anxieties, my laptop had crashed just as I was trying to finish working on important changes to my debut novel that would be published the following year, and I wasn't sure how much, if any, information I had lost in the crash. Not to mention the hundreds of family vacation photos that I hadn't backed up that appeared to be lost as well. I was having ugly fits about my computer issues, so as soon as I dropped off Gillian at her school, I headed off to Richmond, the closest city for emergency tech help, which was a good hour away. I was barely out of town when I got the call from my son.

"I'm fine, Mom," Kyle began. "But an ambulance is taking me to the hospital."

That's one of those declarative sentences you don't ever want to hear, though in hindsight I knew how lucky I was to have heard it from my son, considering how often such a call comes from the police when the accident is far worse.

I whipped around in a U-turn on a two-lane road and raced to get to the high school, which was located right across the street from Gillian's school, before Kyle was taken off to the hospital. I would later learn that he had been walking through the school parking lot when a girl hit him from behind with her car, then proceeded to run him over, but all I could gather as I drove was that Kyle had been injured and an ambulance had been called. I'm a writer, which means I have a pretty vivid imagination; so even though my son was talking to me calmly and coherently, I pictured internal bleeding, debilitating head injuries, the end to athletic pursuits, and no med school for him. Not that he'd planned to go to med school, but still.

My mind flashed through every horrible episode of all the hospital shows I'd seen over the years, from *ER* to *Marcus Welby, M.D.,* and probably even a few from *General Hospital.* I remembered all those "patients" who showed up lucid at the hospital and were wearing toe tags by the end of the program.

Compound this with the requisite amount of parental guilt and angst I was suffering from (*why couldn't I have been there to save him?*), and I was a wreck.

I made it to the school in record time and found Kyle bound onto a spine board—just in case—and being loaded into an ambulance. I wanted to throw up but knew I couldn't do that, nor could I cry. I followed the ambulance to the hospital, where we met Scott and were taken immediately to the front of the triage line. Kyle by then was talking and joking, as if nothing had happened. He wasn't sure what hit him—he said he was walking through the parking lot when he thought a football player friend of his had tackled him from behind.

He had a lot of gravel ground into his knees and elbows, and cuts and abrasions all over. And, mysteriously, tire tracks on his ankle. There's nothing quite so sobering as seeing jeep tracks on your child's skin. We all talked and made light of things while the nurse cleaned him up and we awaited X-rays. The doctor thought he would be okay and wasn't seeing signs of internal bleeding. I wasn't convinced, yet Kyle continued to talk as if he was on speed and just seemed awfully peppy. In fact, his chipper was a little too chipper. Suddenly I saw his face lose all color and the pep vanished in an instant. We caught him just as he was about to hit the ground. Mercifully, it was only an adrenaline crash, and his internal organs seemed to be okay. (There's no accounting for the ten pounds' worth of stress-eating that his passing out at that moment subsequently induced in me, but that's another story.)

Since no one knew why the boy had tire tracks on his ankle and foot, which looked by then precisely like Fred Flinstone's distorted stump of a foot, only purpling up with bruises, they went ahead and X-rayed it. No one could decide whether it was broken or not, so the ER doctor decided it was a sprain and suggested he "challenge it." My son would indeed challenge it eight days later when, in one of those act-first-think-later maneuvers that are the hallmark of teenagers, he impulsively ran in a 5K race, barefoot, after spending the night at a friend's place. All his friends were running in it, so shortly after sunrise, minus appropriate running gear, he took off in borrowed oversize sneakers that he discarded within five minutes and his friend's dad's shorts that were so large he had to fist them in his hand to keep them from falling to the ground. Boys *will* be boys. I was livid, but he survived and his foot, miraculously, seemed okay.

In the days after the accident, details trickled out about what had happened. A girl was text messaging her friend while driving too fast, hit Kyle from behind, then drove over his foot when she kept on going, oblivious of having even hit a human being. He was probably saved much greater injury thanks to his backpack, which was laden as always with thirty pounds' worth of textbooks that absorbed some of the force.

For weeks afterward while Kyle recovered from his injuries, I remained haunted by the incident. I was especially pained to know that he was alone precisely at that moment the car hit him and then drove over him. This knowledge just killed me: that he was there, and I couldn't help him in such a lonely hour. I was probably just across the street dropping off Gillian as it all unfolded. These types of thoughts often plague me when I hear of others' tragedies: innocent victims, people just going about their lives when poof, it all changes. And usually they're alone when they most need someone—or something—to soothe them. A few weeks after the accident, Scott, the kids, and I were at a party with several families, watching a slide show of our vacation photos on somebody's laptop, with an iTunes playlist on as a backdrop. The song "Wonderwall" by Oasis came on.

"Dude, that's the song I was hit by!" my son blurted out to his friends.

Because he was listening to his iPod when he was hit by a car, he has a personal soundtrack—a theme song—for probably the worst thing ever to happen to him.

That my son had a theme song to the accident sort of creeped me out at first, but it didn't bother him. In fact he was happy to hear it playing that night, even though the last time he heard it was under less than ideal circumstances.

I guess I was just glad that in his hour of need, music was there to comfort, and—like that backpack—to soften the blow a little bit. I don't think I'll ever hear that song again without my heart stopping for just a moment, recalling that crucial time I couldn't be there for him. But perhaps when he hears "Wonderwall" my son will remember to be happy he's alive, maybe even be comforted by the music.

~~~~~

I heard that song on the radio recently, and the notion of having a soundtrack to one's life made me start thinking about the soundtrack to my family's collective existence—Graycie's chatter—and how, weirdly, we have been silently and discreetly recorded over the years, in some random manner, by a bird who selectively chooses what she wants to remember in the many, many things she hears us say. The snippets of what she repeats, the "Good night, I love you" she says many nights, the "It's okay" or calling out "Girls!"—they're all relevant to us, all some small but vital component to some of the more mundane but regular parts of our lives. I realized it's sort of fun to have this unusual recording of our family history. Of course it's not permanent; nothing ever is, really. But it's there for now, this creature of ours, this witness to our family history, carrying on our theme in her own unique way.

Conversely, her very chatter serves as the background noise to our lives. We hardly notice her squawks and chirps for the most part. And yet if I'm on the phone with someone and they hear an ear-splitting screech in the background, they're taken aback by the abrupt and loud nature of the sound. What seems a part of normal life to us is very much not the norm to many. Sometimes I yearn for the absence of that noise when it becomes overwhelming, but the truth is, the soundtrack of our lives, courtesy of Graycie, reminds us to be appreciative of one another, and to be grateful for what we have. A daily grace, from Grayce.

CHAPTER 20

If Only I Could Use Her Tail as a Feather Duster

When my kids were very young, I co-opted the obnoxious Barney "Clean Up" song ("Clean up, clean up, everybody do your share") in an effort to diffuse the burden of cleanup. The kids would do their part to pick up their toys, and I was left with the big chores, including the parrot mess. Back then I think I harbored fantasies that one day my much older children would pitch in with the parrot, scrubbing the cage occasionally, or at least wiping up the daily Graycie debris. Oddly, no one ever decided that cleaning up after a filthy parrot fell under the rubric of family duties. Naturally, bird poo grosses them out (me, too, though) and they'll have nothing to do with its eradication.

But at least once they grew older and became relatively self-sufficient, my goal to keep Graycie's cage poop-free became more realistic. (I also try to not eat junk food and avoid anything fattening, and usually that's shot to hell by about ten in the morning, along with the clean birdcage plans.) Years ago such a concept was merely an ambition, rarely fulfilled. But now, I feel like it's more of a mandate. Part of living in a civilized world.

In an *ideal* world I'd thoroughly scrub down the cage every week, with spot cleanings in between. In my reality, well, let's just say that doesn't happen quite so frequently. If I'm home, I'm always on the alert like a Secret Service agent, constantly scanning the parrot zone for bird droppings, partly just because of the desire to try to keep things from getting out of hand, mess-wise, but also to keep ahead of my Labrador, who has been a voracious food mooch ever since she had pups, when she got used to enjoying some twelve cups of homemade dog food each day to keep her puppy-nursing weight up.

When we cut her food allotment back to two meager scoops of dog nuggets, Sassy sought solace in most anything that even simply *appeared* edible. That has included checkbooks left lying around, furnace filters leaning against the wall awaiting installation, a pocket radio, and of course Graycie food castoffs (of which there are plenty, since she drops or throws at least half of what we feed her). Sassy is frequently found with a small, downy feather stuck on the end of her nose, a telltale sign that she's been rooting around the cage in search of goodies. When those aren't at hand, she'll settle for parrot, rabbit, deer, fox, or any other miscellaneous unidentified scat. Sassy is so single-minded in her pursuit of poop that sometimes I have to race her to the cage. On a few occasions, I've slid into home base, hip-checking the dog out of the way to beat her to it, ending up on the floor in my zeal to stop her. The one food she's learned is too unpleasant even for her undiscriminating palate is Graycie's scorching habanero peppers, the discards of which remain where they're dropped until I dispose of them.

Graycie's mess (and perhaps the kids' unwillingness to do the dirty work with it) is particularly annoying when I'm pressed for time. Say, if we're hosting six people for dinner and I am out running errands for that evening. I get back home with enough time to whip everything together, but usually fail to incorporate an hour of bird poop cleanup into my dinner party time-line. This is not at all an unusual scenario. But invariably, ten minutes before guests are slated to arrive, I am on my hands and knees like Cinderella, scrubbing parrot crap. A good gauge of how close a friend is to me is how messy the cage is when one comes to visit. Our closest friends often see the *real* parrot cage in its nasty natural state; we probably give other, less familiar guests the false impression that parrots are very clean creatures.

It's not enough that parrots are incredibly messy; their slop is also extremely difficult to clean up. Parrot scat dries quickly and is amazingly stubborn stuff. So I usually try to incorporate a spritz bath for the bird with cursory poop cleanup, filling a large pump spray bottle with warm water, then aiming it at Graycie, who has a sort of love-hate relationship with a bath. If I don't bathe her regularly, she'll take a bird bath in her water bowl and then she'll be out of water when she's stuck in the cage and we're not home. My girls actually enjoy pitching in when it comes time to bathe the bird—they love to spray Graycie because she gets so into the rhythm of the pump bottle and bobs her head to the beat, clucking along as well, sometimes hooting a tune. It's always entertaining. However, while Graycie loves being showered with water and the pumping sound, she hates the water bottle itself, and if I get too close with it she tries to attack it and me, which puts an end to the fun.

Parrots naturally have a lot of dander, and spray baths keep the level of parrot dust from overwhelming the area in which the bird is housed. So after spraying her for about five minutes, I then have to deal with the large puddle of dander-, food-, and poop-filled water all along the base of the cage (the girls are long gone by the time this is necessary). Allowing the entire mess on the floor to soak up for several minutes simplifies the task, which usually takes a good handful of paper towels and sturdy rubber gloves. It's about a twenty-minute cleanup, during which I have to be ever vigilant that I'm not dive-bombed by yet more poop. I can say with pride I've yet to be pooped on from above, although I've come close on several occasions, and a few times Gillian's tugged me out of the way just in the nick of time. And of course while I'm at the foot of the cage scrubbing, hovering right above me like a stooped turkey vulture is Graycie, on the prowl, waiting for me to be engrossed enough in my cleaning quest to forget that she's there, at which point she grabs a hank of my hair and rips.

The cost of cleanup is not simply measured in time and dignity. It comes with an unbelievable amount of Bounty (the quicker picker upper), as well. I'm not great at math, so forgive me if my calculations are a grotesque exaggeration, but I recently tried to tally up a rough guesstimate of how many paper towels I go through cleaning up after the parrot each year, and I've deduced that it's about a hundred and eighty rolls. There is some sort of irony when I consider how many trees must have died to create enough paper towels for us to clean up after Graycie, whereas had she remained in the wild she'd have lived in those trees and messed right on them and it would probably have been healthful for the trees instead of leading to their decimation.

Parrot excrement is truly amazing stuff. It's so strong and resistant to eradication that it would be the perfect adhesive to salvage your favorite broken china cup from Auntie Mabel's tea set. In addition, I think it would make a fine grout. Although we'd need to convince people that kelly green is a desirable color for grout. I saw on the Internet that someone's already figured out how to flack sea bird guano for fertilizer. Lest we forget, poop is poop is poop. But with a little marketing, anything is possible.

Over the years I've purchased all sorts of products that ostensibly help to eradicate bird poop: scrubbers, enzymes, you name it. Although I have yet to attempt the parrot flight suit—no joking, it's like a birdie jumpsuit, usually in the guise of some sort of schlocky costume, complete with a poop pouch. I figure Graycie would shred that getup in two seconds, tops, and while it might well do the trick for some birds, there's something a bit undignified about the whole thing. It's bad enough the bird's held hostage in a cage with clipped wings, but to add insult to injury, you make the poor bird wear a disco suit or dress it up like Fred Astaire in a faux tuxedo? Yeah, I don't think the parrot flight suit is in our bird's future.

Though if it came in a straitjacket version, I might be tempted.

CHAPTER 21

It's a Girl! Wait—It's a Boy!
No—It's an Egg!

At about age sixteen, right when Kyle started associating "Wonderwall" with tire tracks on his body, Graycie began acting awfully pissy. If I didn't know better, I'd have attributed it to PMS. But we didn't even know if she was female, so the verdict was still out. She'd gone from a rather agreeable several-year stretch of not being too ornery to suddenly aiming for the jugular whenever I was in her presence. I couldn't figure out what could have precipitated this change of heart. I started thinking maybe it was simply teenage oppositional defiance—I was seeing plenty of that with my own teens, so certainly it seemed within the realm of possibility. Then again, so did the PMS, so what did I know?

I kept complaining to my good friend Tana about Graycie's habit of pulling out newspapers from the bottom of the cage and shredding them all over the floor. And how she'd get a maniacal glint in her eyes in my presence and then *whoosh*, she'd strike out at me like a surly cobra, attempting to peck/

bite/gnaw at any piece of me onto which she could latch with that beak. I was convinced she needed some sort of anger management therapy. Or perhaps *she* was really a *he* and was tired of being called a girl?

"I think it's some bizarre teen-related thing," I said to Tana. "You know how people adopt little baby chimpanzees and they're so cute and cuddly and then they turn into psycho killers once they hit their teen years and reach sexual maturity?"

"You hit the nail on the head," Tana said. "That bird of yours needs to get laid!"

All I ever heard about African grays' social tendencies was that they don't even want other parrot company, so I presumed Graycie was happy flying solo. But it does seem to be a biological mandate to proliferate, even (or especially) when it comes to grasshoppers or sand fleas or protozoa. So why would my parrot not want to get in on the action?

Of course there wasn't much I could do about this. There was no way in hell I would try to borrow someone's African gray in a pillowcase for a romance-infused little weekend tête-à-tête. My animal husbandry days were long behind me. So, shy of any direct evidence that Graycie was on the manhunt, I was going to keep on blaming teen angst. This worked fine when it came to my kids, and as far as I knew they weren't in search of a mate. Besides, even if they were, about the *last* person they'd clue in to that information would be me. What self-respecting teen ever informs their parents of their intentions? Surely, like the teen she was, my parrot would keep that one to herself as well.

In the meantime, I had to stop the bird from shredding, so I would frequently keep her in her cage during her waking hours, something she didn't appreciate. If her cage was uncovered and I didn't open it within eight minutes' time, the bird retaliated in full force. First she would begin to pluck on a single bar in her cage. She'd keep that up, every five seconds or so, for a good ten minutes, until I was ready to bash my head against the wall. If that didn't work, she'd start dragging her beak across the bars, the disgruntled prisoner rattling a tin cup against the bars of the county jail. Our very own jailbird.

Next she'd go to the bottom of the cage, which is made up of another type of metal and has bars running crisscross across it to catch droppings onto the newspapers. She'd grab a rung of the rack with her beak and try to forcefully pry it, much like tightening a lug nut with pliers, which made a sound like fingernails on a chalkboard. If I didn't know better I'd have thought she'd learned her torture techniques from KGB operatives. But which one of us was really being held hostage? Me or the bird?

She was letting her presence be known in a big way, and I was at her mercy.

At the height of her discontent, I went away to a writing conference for about six days. It was a chance to mingle with other writers and network, while escaping those annoying little have-to's like cleaning up after parrots that can make day-to-day life somewhat hellish. Usually when I'm away Graycie gets her daily allotment of food and water but the paper doesn't seem to get changed out much and generally no one bothers to deal with her complicated upkeep. In the division of labor, my husband gets to do taxes and take out the trash and I get to wipe up bird doo-doo, so I guess it's a pretty fair trade-off. But I was ready for a parrot-free couple of days.

When I got home late Sunday night from my trip, everyone was already in bed. The next morning when I uncovered

Graycie's cage, I glanced down to see what appeared to be the cracked, bloody remains of an egg—an egg!—with a few bits of shell here and there, scattered on the cage floor.

Now I do like to introduce new foods to Graycie, most of which she flatly rejects. I'm usually the only one who does this; maybe my husband will give her some leftover apple at breakfast time, but the kids? Never. And in a million years I couldn't imagine anyone offering up *raw egg* to the bird.

"Okay, people, who fed Graycie eggs?" I shouted. "I mean it's kind of sick, offering up an egg to a bird. It's like feeding them their young!"

My kids just shrugged.

"I didn't give her anything!" Scott insisted.

It was a mystery. Somehow that egg got there, and I was going to get to the bottom of it. I bundled up the messy papers from the catch pan in the cage and for the next day or so held vigil for some sort of evidence to appear, like the image of the Virgin Mary materializing on a piece of burnt toast.

In the meantime, Graycie had stepped up her shredding to a frenzy. It had gotten to the point that I had to stop opening her cage altogether because the minute I did, she'd race to the top, get in a few rapid attack swipes my way, then race along the outside of the cage to where the bottom tray held the mess-catching newspaper. Once there she would begin the delicate excision of poop-encrusted newspaper. She'd pull one sheet at a time, grasping the page in one foot and ripping off and shredding it with her mouth until a mound of filthy paper piled up on the floor. I was spending hours sweeping up after her, only to have her immediately mess things up all over again, often with a flourish of flapped wings.

When she grew bored of shredding paper, she'd just drop

off the cage for a walkabout through the house. She's a stealthy bird, and often I'd have no clue she was no longer on the cage until the silence became too apparent. Sometimes she'd slip off, wander around, start chewing on the shoe molding along the baseboard, and then yell at herself in my voice, "Graycie! Stop it! Bad girl!" (The funniest part is, I don't think I've ever said "Bad girl!" to her, only to the dogs when they're trying to eat the parrot. So it shows how very intelligent African grays are that she can extrapolate the usage of that word to something she knew she ought not be doing.)

For about two days I smugly thought I'd outwitted her. I'd trudged down to the basement and dragged up the unwieldy "baby play yard," which consists of about five three-foot square segments of plastic fencing that can be formed into a large circle in which to trap wayward toddlers trying to flee their confines. With a toddlerlike teen parrot in our midst, I had to revert to the olden days.

I set up the play yard with a perimeter that extended into much of the usable space in our living room. It almost seemed as if Graycie was perfectly content to wander around the floor within the zone, until I looked up one evening while watching TV with the kids to see her perched atop the upper edge of the fence. Why I wouldn't have figured out earlier that she could easily scale the thing I don't know. And of course scale it she did, while also trailing poop all over the molded plastic grids.

One day I couldn't find Graycie anywhere and panic set in. After searching through the main floor of the house, I was ready to look upstairs, though I couldn't fathom how her little birdie legs would get her up the steps. I was about to lose it when I heard a rustling noise and looked over to see she'd somehow wedged her way into an empty shoe box one of the kids had left on the floor. She seemed extremely happy inside her little fort, and was chomping away at the cardboard, so I let her stay there, even when she said, "C'mon, Gray, go in your cage." (She knows the deal.)

Soon we started placing empty boxes on the ground near her cage, because then at least she'd stick nearby and busy herself with shredding cardboard instead of chewing through electrical cords. The broom and I became even more intimately acquainted during this stint.

When she was stuck in her cage, though, she would cower in the corner, perched atop her water bowl, shivering, her feathers semi-ruffled. And if she wasn't cowering, she was in protest mode: plinking metal bars, determined that if she was going to be unhappy, then damnit, so was I.

And then, a few days later, I uncovered Graycie and voilà, yet another broken egg had magically appeared on the floor of the cage. This time the shell was intact enough for me to see that it was not bigger than a walnut.

I felt sort of stupid, because I had until then simply assumed that where there was an egg, there would have to be a male bird contributing to the output. I clearly missed the day they went over parrot sex in health class. So that morning I made a couple of important discoveries. First of all, my bird was officially a female. And second of all, she was perfectly capable of laying eggs without the benefit of a boy bird (not to mention illicit behavior in the backseat of a car). On top of that I realized that I was entirely out of my league with this one: What do you do when your bird starts dropping raw eggs from high atop her perch in the middle of the night?

This called for the big guns, so I reached out to our old parrot vet, Dr. Stahl, via e-mail and spoke with his assistant, Jen.

She kindly advised me to strongly discourage any more egg laying. Jen told me that the more eggs the bird lays, the less healthy it is for the creature, because making and laying eggs is physically exhausting and can drain the bird of proper nutrients. Worse still, parrots can become egg-bound, with an egg lodged somewhere up there (wherever "there" was—it was hard to tell with all those feathers in the way), which could result in death.

"So how, pray tell, does one encourage a feisty parrot with a mind of her own to stop laying eggs?" I asked.

"You have to make her uncomfortable in her cage," she said. "You want to discourage the nesting instinct, so no paper shredding. Move the cage to an unfamiliar location, and do anything that will make her feel it's not the right place to lay a clutch of eggs."

So just like Jed Clampett loading up the truck and moving to Beverly, we packed up the cage and moved Graycie to another area of the house. She had no more paper to shred, no fun toys (because sometimes parrots mistake toys for a mate), no spiffy empty boxes to nest in. And she was pissed. So imagine my dismay when another egg showed up two days later, despite my bird's anxiety levels reaching high proportions.

This time I noticed bits of shell completely missing. Apparently she'd taken to eating her, uh, output. Granted, they say shells contain a lot of calcium, and popping out a clutch of eggs depletes one's calcium stores, but eating your own eggs? Come on!

I kept having visions of finding my parrot egg-bound and belly-up on the floor of the cage one morning. Thankfully, after egg number three, Graycie lost the desire to birth any more. That one must've been in the oven by the time we'd moved her cage. When I asked Jen if my friend Tana had been right all along—that Graycie's moodiness was simply because she wanted to get laid—she told me she wasn't far off base.

"Parrots can get broody when they're about to lay eggs," she said. Broody equals moody. Moody we were used to—we did have teens, after all. Turns out Graycie was basically suffering from birdie PMS after all. Who'd have known? I couldn't help but think that teenage oppositional defiance would have been a much more agreeable diagnosis, because eventually teens outgrow it. Although heaven help us when birdie menopause kicks in.

CHAPTER 22

Beware the Evil Snowman

After the egg laying episodes, Graycie became a little more agreeable. Not exactly to the point that she wanted to hug us and thank us for taking care of her, but a little less confrontational. But we knew that something had to give. It was no wonder she was bored: she'd spent all those years stuck in that cage. And even when she could get out of it, her horizons were pretty limited. The thing is, I didn't blame her for her retaliatory behavior—I'd do the same thing. Nevertheless, we seemed to have reached an impasse. And I really hate impasses.

One particular thing that was vexing me was Graycie's continued dismounting of the cage with hapless abandon. My husband has the naive tendency to trust all our pets (whereas I feel like the zookeeper who needs to keep all under a watchful eye), and he would leave the bird up on the open perch on her cage—unattended—and go off to work.

On many occasions, I'd remind him she needed to be contained. "Uh, the bird snuck off the cage again," I'd say. "You *have* to close her up if you're going downstairs!"

"Oh, she's fine," he'd reply. Such a softie for the bird, but then who had to deal with the repercussions?

I think he felt guilty about imprisoning her. Plus, when she was imprisoned she acted like an ornery prisoner, and Scott bore the brunt of her bad behavior, since the banging, clanging, and all-around annoying noises were seemingly amplified through the floor into his office, which I don't doubt is slightly distracting when on a business phone call.

But left alone to roam, Graycie just waited till she knew he'd rounded the corner before she was doing a triple back gainer off the damned cage and onto the floor to go exploring uncharted territories. Our own little Admiral Robert Peary. Often her first stop was our once nicely upholstered living room chair that had a sort of monkey/jungle scene on it. I should have known she'd think it was a great place to start chewing through fabric in search of stuffing that can be shredded. And that was just the beginning.

I can't emphasize enough that parrots might be incredibly smart but they do lack common sense. Graycie's intellect is probably akin to that of a precocious toddler. And would you leave a really smart two-year-old on her own in a house? No way. This would be like when my little brother Rob was three and my mother decided to nap when he napped, but instead of napping he got up, walked out the front door, crossed several busy roads, and found his way down to the fire station a quarter mile away, where he got to see his favorite shiny red fire truck.

You can't trust these little buggers; they've got their own ill-conceived agendas. Besides which, always lurking, just like those ominous French horns in *Peter and the Wolf,* is our own little wolfie, Bridget, who even *looks* like a wolf and has clearly and repeatedly demonstrated the desire to chow down on our bird. I have imagined coming home one day to my dog leaning back, cross-legged, fangs a-gleaming, picking a Graycie feather from her teeth with a tiny parrot rib bone. It would be just like her. One day I came home to discover the cage open and the bird nowhere to be found (certainly not in the unattended cage). I took the absence of blood or tufts of feather remains as a positive sign that she hadn't necessarily met with foul play—at least not of the canine fashion. Again I went on a search, to no avail.

Maybe ten minutes later, I heard grumbling sounds. Not discernible words, but something akin to a distant conversation. I followed the noises and found myself facing the parrot cabinet. The parrot cabinet is a floor-level cabinet containing four shelves that butts up to our kitchen island. This is where we store things relevant to the bird. We also toss in things that might be needed at the nearby dining room table, or that we can't figure out what else to do with. Thus you'll find inside a bag of parrot chow, the Dremel for trimming her claws, old toys with which she's grown bored, a package of hot chili peppers (a favorite of hers), the sheet with which we cover her at night, a bowl of peanuts, and, randomly, a bowl full of colored chalk (this went with a spiffy set of chalkboard place mats that once seemed like such a good idea but failed to contain my then younger children's sloppy eating habits and only distracted them from mealtime).

I opened the cabinet and who did I find, lurking in the dark on the bottom shelf, but Graycie. As soon as I opened the cabinet door, she whistled a catcall (to which I always reply, "Hel-loooo, gooooood lookin'!") and she stepped right out as if she was getting out of an elevator. I haven't the slightest idea how she got in, or how she got the door shut behind her. And

I probably don't want to know. Apparently while inside, she'd just played around with a bunch of small wooden shapes (parrot toys she would never play with in the cage, so we'd stuck them in the cabinet), surprisingly not destroying a thing.

Another time I came home to find her right in front of the cabinet with the door ajar, wandering around the scattered remains of the colored chalk that she'd pulled out of the bowl and all over the floor, leaving a trail of colorful chalky footprints in her wake.

During this wandering phase, my biggest fear was that Graycie would get to the nearby sliding glass door, find it ajar (which it sometimes is), and keep on going. Originally we had a fully functional screen door there, but our dingo dog busted through it with such regularity that we finally stopped bothering to fix it.

One day I had a stroke of genius that I was sure was a marvelous solution to her *Hogan's Heroes* escape attempts. Graycie is very particular about things: she doesn't care for strange objects being introduced into her environment. God forbid I put a new toy in her cage; instead it must be gradually introduced or it will be forever shunned. I first have to set it in a somewhat close proximity to her cage—not too close, but close enough to be within her sight line. If it's too close, she gets stressed out. Then little by little I move it closer to her, until she accepts it. I figured that if I put something near the cage with which she wasn't familiar, maybe it would discourage her curiosity.

I looked around for something I could easily move, and settled on a life-size fiberfill snowman that stood sentry in my front hall from December until I remembered to put it away. (We were well past winter.)

The day I put my plan into action was a Saturday. It was afternoon, but my teens were still asleep and I'd hoped to keep it that way, since they all get so sleep-deprived with school activities and such. The house was remarkably silent, in fact, until I picked up the snowman and started to carry it toward the cage. The instant Graycie spotted it she began emitting a frighteningly loud, shrill distress call that I'm sure in parrotese meant something along the lines of "Holy shit! Man the torpedoes!" The sound was like nothing I'd heard out of her in all her years, and she repeated it over and over, like a car alarm (which of course triggered the dogs to bark as well). Clearly the snowman would keep the bird from coming off the cage; sadly, it would've led to heart failure if I didn't move it back pronto. *So much for my brilliant idea,* I thought.

But you know what? For a brief period after that she was a little less inclined to escape quite so regularly. Fear of the evil snowman lurking in the distance just might have temporarily done the trick.

One solid yet unwelcome bit of advice Dr. Stahl's office had given us when Graycie started behaving badly was that we would have to start from scratch to try to get her to be a more cooperative parrot. This would mean reverting to the training techniques we thought we'd gotten past some sixteen years earlier: holding her on a wooden dowel, having her climb from one dowel to another, and eventually working up to having her climb on one of our hands and then going back and forth from hand to hand.

The problem with this plan was twofold. One: doing that dowel-to-dowel thing doesn't work anymore, because the minute I've got her on a dowel, she scurries down to my end of the stick lightning-fast and bites me. And two: we seem to attract dominant pets (see: our dog Bridget), and I've dealt with them long enough to realize that they have these wily ways of circumventing the intent of the training exercises. It's almost as if they've got their little claws crossed, like, "I'll fake it that I'm cooperating but I'm totally not holding to this and when it comes time I'll do what I damn well please." Which is a little frustrating when you're supposed to be the boss.

Kids do the same thing, don't they? But at least you can hold the car keys out as a lure for cooperative behavior. What's Graycie got to lose with her defiant behavior? Not a whole hell of a lot. Maybe some peanuts from me, but then she just gets them when Scott caves to her. So I assumed the relearning old tricks treatment wasn't going to work.

We briefly considered taking Graycie to an animal behaviorist whose goal is to help parrot owners correct untoward behaviors in their birds so that the birds aren't either hated or abandoned. This is a lofty goal and one with which I was in agreement. Until I learned that the hourly rate (in the hundreds of dollars) for the behaviorist was way out of our price range. It may seem insensitive or even shortsighted, but we were facing college tuition for three kids, so money was a consideration. So the parrot shrink wasn't gonna happen.

Yet here we were with the most uncooperative of parrots, bent on making our lives a little slice of hell pie with a cherry on top if and when she wasn't happy, which appeared to be during far too many waking hours.

We'd clearly entered into new territory with Graycie, and it was relatively hostile terrain, by comparison to earlier in her life. It was as if she wanted us to know damn well that she was tired of the terms of her tenure in our household, and changes would be afoot if she had anything to say about it. I think if she and Bridget had spoken the same language they'd have easily allied themselves with each other and fomented a revolution in our home. Shy of being able to do that, it seems as if the two instead waged a steady ground campaign against us. (Bridget is a master escape artist as well, enjoying her own frequent walkabouts throughout the neighborhood. The "stubborn dog" electric fence collar we had to resort to in order to contain the dog is so powerful that the first time Bridget willfully breached it, she let out such a loud yelp that Graycie continues to repeat it still—a reminder to us or to her?)

Graycie's wanderlust and general need to cause trouble reminded me of a wayward child who has grown up to behave in a manner aimed at spiting the parents. And I could appreciate this to a certain extent, except that we'd been fairly liberal in how we'd managed the parrot, but for the limitations she'd set up in the relationship (i.e., the savagery part). So her lashing out at our keeping her locked up seemed sort of cockeyed, when we kept her locked up because she behaved in such a way that demanded that we so do.

I was stumped.

CHAPTER 23

The Tree of Life (Graycie's, That Is)

Sure, our parrot had turned into a vengeful and troublesome teen—she would probably be out scoring crack if she were human and had keys to the car—but we weren't ready to give up. We'd grown a bit used to her behavior and learned some diversionary tricks for dealing with her. However, we wanted to have reached more than a compromise—ideally, Graycie would be happy and not whiling away her hours in a state of ceaseless boredom.

The summer after the egg laying, we all road-tripped for an annual get-together with my brother Joe, his wife, Sandy, who was a dear friend of mine from college, and their children. Because we all graduated from Penn State, we made our annual trip back to State College a family tradition, and the kids always looked forward to it.

About forty minutes outside of our destination, we drove by a van parked in the driveway of what looked a bit like a haunted house. On the sides of the van were large magnetic signs with pictures of African gray parrots advertising parrot trees.

"Wait! We've got to turn around!" I told Scott. "There's a parrot van back there—I have to see what it's all about."

We were already running late and hadn't planned for any diversions. Scott thought I was slightly mad, but with a little additional lobbying from the kids, he humored us and turned the car around and drove slowly back so I could read the phone number on the sign. Then we pulled into a nearby driveway and I called the number to ask if we could stop to check out these mysterious parrot trees. I told the man who answered that we'd be there in ten seconds.

The tattered Victorian home looked as if it had seen better days, and from the outside appeared to have been the scene of a wild fraternity party, with large trash bags filled with beer can empties littering the space beneath the back deck. We heard the distinctive sound of talking parrots before we even climbed the steps up to the porch, where we found the owner, a legless and somewhat grizzled man, sitting in a wheelchair with an African gray and a green parrot perched on either shoulder, looking like some sort of landlubber pirate. Empty beer cans were everywhere, and a traveling parrot groomer was nearby trimming a bird's claws. The kids and I could only talk to one another with our eyes as we glanced around at the place.

"Yikes," Kendall finally whispered to me.

"No doubt," I said.

Compared to this place, ours would win the *Good House-keeping* award by a landslide (and that's saying something, considering I spent an inordinate amount of time cleaning Graycie's home, yet very little cleaning my own).

The man warmly welcomed us, set down his beer, and wheeled into the house to show us his wares. We stepped into his large living room, which was slightly pungent with aroma de parrot. Dust motes swirled through the beams of late-day sun streaming through the stained-glass pentagram window in the gabled roof peak, illuminating some forty handcrafted trees of varying sizes. Each tree was assembled atop a wheeled platform and constructed from the branches of manzanita trees, all intermingled with tufts of sparkly cotton "snow," miniature village pieces, and twinkling lights: Christmas decorations. Christmas in July.

His birds certainly seemed to be very happy hanging out on the trees—could it be possible that Graycie would actually like such a thing, not turn on her squawk alarm and freak out the neighbors? And would those branches last in the presence of an über-destructive parrot who has chewed through soft wood perches in a couple of hours?

The answer to the second question, the man assured us, was yes. The first was a crapshoot. We choked at the price— it was more than the cost of the parrot shrink we'd briefly considered—and then mulled it over. Among other considerations, we hadn't the slightest idea how to get a five-foot by four-foot tree home with all five of us already wedged in the minivan. Finally we told him we'd ponder it over the weekend. Over the next couple of days our kids lobbied for the tree, convinced it was precisely what Graycie needed (even though I still think a boy bird would've solved her problem—while increasing ours exponentially).

"Think how much fun Grayce would have on that tree," Kendall said. "If I was a parrot it's exactly what I'd want."

"Please, can't we please get it for her?" Gillian implored. "It's awesome."

"You guys! It's a *tree*!" I said. "It'll be smack in the middle of our house. One more thing to be messy and yucky. And right by the kitchen!"

"It is kind of cool," Kyle said.

"I don't know if we can even fit it in the car," Scott added. This was a weak argument. Cage shower notwithstanding, the kids all knew the man has the spatial skills of a Russian matrushka doll designer, and can fit practically anything anywhere. His car packing feats are the stuff of legend in our household. If anyone could fit that damned tree in our car, it was my husband.

Sure enough, two days later, on the return trip, we diverted to the home of the parrot tree man and picked up Graycie's new home. One she might flatly reject, leaving us out a few hundred bucks. The kids endured the six-hour drive wedged uncomfortably between the sharp branches of the tree, their contribution toward the salvation of our very bored bird. Clearly we were desperate.

We took it slowly introducing Graycie to the tree, first placing it clear across the room in which she resided, at a safe distance in case she went nuts over it. Each day we inched it closer toward her, finally butting it up against her cage. By then her curiosity had gotten the better of her, and she couldn't help but explore this new object. She climbed aboard and was immediately sold on it. We weren't too keen on marring the center of our home with a tree we knew would end up being absolutely filthy, especially when we'd already gone to great lengths to build a zone in our house that could accommodate the parrot (who knew she'd outwit us in that venture?). But we were so weary of trying to figure out ways in which we could keep the bird somewhat contented that we had to relent. It was that or put up with perpetual bad behavior.

Soon the tree became her favorite place, and it was as if the storm broke and the clouds parted to allow through a beckoning sunshine. We loaded the tree up with foraging toys in which she could search for and find food, and she spends most of her time hanging out on the thing, sometimes sleeping peacefully with her head turned around and tucked comfortably into her feathers, other times whittling the ends of branches into very fine points. I hope she's sharpening the tree tips for fun, rather than channeling Madame Defarge, quietly knitting her death registry (nay, an executioner whetting his blade), waiting with calculated patience for the day in which it will finally be called upon.

For a good stretch of time, the parrot tree seemed to have solved our problems. But life is not static, and Graycie is already growing bored again. How ironic that we've raised our children—who are finally emerging from the occasionally obstinate teen years—to become free and independent, but we will be indefinitely placating this intelligent toddler/teen parrot, who perhaps because of her lack of freedom is doomed to continue to behave in this contrary way.

CHAPTER 24

Handling the Hot Potato

While Graycie has her charming moments, her darker side always wants to assert itself, making physically managing her challenging at best, and excruciatingly painful at worst. Handling a fiery-tempered wild parrot is a lot like juggling with samurai swords—it can be pulled off with a lot of skill and confidence, but without that skill and confidence, it can be a disaster. And the older Graycie gets, the wilier she becomes.

For instance: Scott and I recently indulged ourselves with a quick overnight with our good friends Gary and Tana (fortunately our kids are old enough now that we can take off and leave them in charge at home). This much-needed getaway included sailing on their boat near the Chesapeake Bay. As we were admiring the clever names of the boats tethered at a nearby marina, I came up with the most likely title for my vessel, if I ever got one.

"So what do you think of this?" I asked them. "Grayce Escape."

No one got it at first.

"Grayce, as in Graycie," I said. I'd become so frustrated with Graycie's recent lapse into the world of unacceptable parrot behavior (the tree didn't solve *all* of our problems), and I was relishing being away from her for twenty-four parrot-free hours. "The boat would be my chance to escape Grayce."

They all laughed.

Not five minutes later I got a call from Kendall.

"Grrrrrrrrrr!" she huffed.

"Oh no, what's wrong?"

"It's Graycie," she said. "I felt badly about her being stuck in the cage, so I opened it up and put her on the tree. I went upstairs to do some homework and I came down and—"

I could easily fill in the blanks. Parrot, walkabout, cabinet, won't return to cage.

"She's climbing up the shelves now, Mom," Kendall moaned.

It sounded like the parrot was headed for the kitchen counter, a first. This required quick thinking, and we had to trust that Kendall would be able to manage Graycie, who rarely has intentions of being manageable.

Kendall was especially fearful of Graycie's wrath, so I couldn't put her in a position to be victimized by the bird, yet she wanted to leave the house to meet a friend and couldn't just leave the parrot wandering around alone. For one futile second I wished she hadn't taken pity on the bird by letting her out; we always tell the kids to leave her locked up if they don't think they can get her back in when necessary. But then I shifted my focus back to the problem at hand and instructed Ken to find the barbecue tools, the ones with the really long handles.

By now Graycie was sitting in a wicker basket on the top shelf of the cabinet.

"Take the long-handled spatula and shove it underneath the basket," I told Kendall. "And the long-armed tongs? Try to clasp the upper edge of the basket with that. But before you do this, go open the cage door, close the upper perch, and move the cage near the basket so you can just dump the bird in, okay?"

This was like trying to explain over the phone to a novice cook how to prepare a soufflé.

I hung up the phone so Kendall would have two free hands to complete her rescue mission.

A few minutes later she called back.

"You should've seen it," Kendall said, laughing. "Oh, my god. That bird is going to be terrified of tongs for the rest of her life."

Kendall got her out of the cabinet fairly easily, but then Graycie flapped her wings so hard the basket fell to the ground, and Kendall had to grab the whole thing lickety split and dump the basket and Graycie into the cage. Then she had to close the cage with the tongs, because the entire time the parrot was gouging her beak through the rungs of the cage trying to bite her hand.

So much for my Grayce Escape, eh?

~~~~~

While the kids could finally be trusted to survive—and behave—without parental supervision, Graycie was clearly going to be our perpetual problem child. However, we've noticed various parallels between our parrot and our children over the years, with their entering adolescence at around the same time, and constantly challenging us, testing our limits and how much unacceptable behavior we will tolerate. Except with Graycie, it seems that with age has not come any mellowing, or any sense of acceptance of us as, if not her friends, then at least allies. Teens, at some point, usually come to at least somewhat accept their parents. Our parrot? Not so much. Each year it seems she devises more and more ways to attack, outwit, and outmaneuver us in order to achieve her goals.

It frustrates me that while we've met with reasonable success in parenthood—i.e., maintaining the upper hand in the relationships with our kids—Scott and I have failed miserably in parrothood—i.e., the state in which one must sustain a healthy and happy (and cooperative) parrot.

Our kids (almost) always responded well to authority. Graycie? Not so much. Usually she just looks at us with a cold stare that says, "You know I could snap your finger in half easier than it is for you to break a Lorna Doone in two." And she means it.

The parental ploys, the "all that I've done for you over the years" manipulations that one can usually exploit with blood relatives, don't work. (And in her case, all we've done over the years is plenty. Or far too much, depending on how you look at it.) It's vexing that we can't employ the full range of human emotions upon the bird as we can with a dog or cat—with Graycie, hugging, touching, or any form of physical contact is strongly discouraged. Perhaps I'm anthropomorphizing by assuming my bird *wants* to be touched—for that matter, her behavior sort of proves just the opposite—but isn't mutual, unconditional love supposed to be the biggest perk in the pet/owner relationship?

During a visit to the vet last year, during which we happily discovered that our new vet had been a veterinary assistant for Dr. Stahl when Graycie was young, the doctor mentioned that African grays will cry red tears when stressed. Graycie, who was at that moment having her claws filed, indeed had red moisture pooling in her eyes. Were it any other creature in my house, I'd be snuggling up and trying to make it all better. But with Graycie? Not gonna happen. She's too guarded; I'm too terrified. It's really difficult to bond with a pet when the animal refuses to accept kindness, let alone be affectionate in return. It's sort of like dealing with a sullen teen who's bent on rejecting your kindnesses and moral support no matter what the circumstances. The concept of unconditional love doesn't apply.

When I explained to the vet how I was terrified to hold the bird for various and sundry reasons, she replied, "I don't blame you. I wouldn't want her perched on my shoulder! Her beak is right there!" So I've got empathy from a professional at least. *Yes, Mrs. Gardiner, you aren't crazy. You're not a bad mother. Really, you're not,* I keep telling myself.

But Graycie does come in handy sometimes. Just about every time I put the dogs out, she reminds them as a courtesy, "Don't bark!" And her capacity to charm me when I least expect it holds her in good stead. After biting me in the morning, at bedtime she'll make her loud kissing smack and say, "Good night. I love you," and just as quickly as I'm about to unearth the slow cooker for her I'm back to being fond of the crazy bird.

We also have our shared interests. For instance, Graycie

and I like to sing together. Often I'll just wander by her cage and start singing sentences to her and she joins in, in that low conversational chatter she loves. It makes no sense, but we're almost harmonizing, in a precious moment of bonding. Frequently, I'll walk by her cage and she'll do the first half of a wolf whistle, which I'll finish off. Like a couple that finish each other's sentences, we can almost predict each other's actions. It can be sort of eerie, actually. Other times she surprises me by asking "Whatssamatter?" when something actually is the matter, like she knows it from my tone of voice, or has heard me if I've been crying. Omniscient parrot? Spy? Sociopath? You decide.

Plus, Graycie and I have lots of inside jokes. Like when I speak to her in my entirely corrupted Italian superlatives—making up words by adding the suffix "issimo," which makes something the best, in Italian.

"Good morrrrrning, Gray!" Graycie will say first thing in the morning to me, drawing out the word "morning" into three or four syllables. Or she'll say, "Morning! Hey, how are ya?," sounding a bit like Curly from the Three Stooges.

To which I'll reply, "How are you, my piccola bellissima pappagallissima?," calling her the small most beautiful most parrot, which of course makes not one whit of sense and for which Italian speakers would have my head. Graycie will usually respond with a catcall. And at my age, I'm perfectly happy to elicit catcalls from parrots, since no one else is bothering to whistle at me. So maybe she justifies her presence simply through unsolicited flattery. Vanity, thy name is woman, after all.

Sometimes I feel like I'm playing by the rules of traditional warfare against an enemy combatant who doesn't respect those standards. I'm going about it as if Graycie is a rational-thinking human being, when in fact, she is a wild parrot. I suppose I need to think like a parrot, but how does one do that? And in any case, I do know this: what she prefers most is to wound me. When I clear the paper from the cage, she races down to attack. When I reach to open the perch on top, she's there before I complete the job, waiting to take a chomp. If I step around the back of the cage to get the water dish, she scurries across the top, situating herself beak-to-nose with me so that I have to practically do a backbend to avoid the snapping beak. Graycie is to her cage what pit bulls are to darkened junkyards. And when she sneaks off the cage on those frequent surreptitious meanderings, she attacks my ankles and feet as I try to catch her and return her to her perch. I can't control her. That old adage about not biting the hand that feeds simply does not apply to my parrot. If only I could redirect her energy toward positive beak usage—maybe wood carving, or ice sculpture—my life would be so much easier.

Sometimes when Graycie is unbearably irascible, I will put her in a time-out. This involves wheeling her cage into the front hall, which puts her just far enough away that she can't see what's going on in the rest of the main floor of the house. Occasionally this is the perfect solution. And the change of scenery results in my getting some much-needed peace and quiet. However, for the most part, when I put her in the front hall she tends to get chatty. She'll chirp, squawk, whistle a little bit, and conduct mini-conversations with herself. And the irony is, in those moments, her absence makes my heart grow fonder. How can you stay angry at a bird who is in the middle of yelling at your children (who aren't even there), "That's one, two, time-out!"?

This affinity for talking when she thinks no one's listening is just yet another way she defies our wishes and expectations. Invariably when we have guests over, the first thing they request is talking on demand. And Graycie will *never* speak when she's expected to. Summertime is usually the best time for parrot entertainment, because we can take our friends out on the back deck, close enough that she can hear us but not see us. Once we get engrossed in our own conversations, then and only then will she get to chattering, often adding little *"hrrrr, hrrrr, hrrrr"* chuckles that make me think Dick Cheney must be nearby. Yet the minute she knows we've all stopped to listen to her, she ceases with her talk. If we hadn't had enough witnesses to her conversational prowess within the family over the years, I'd easily be accused of having concocted her intelligence.

~~~~~~~

Each day when I put food and water in Graycie's bowls, I know I'm an involuntary player in an eternal game of chicken, trying to stay one step ahead of her as she races over to grip the bowl with muscles behind that beak as powerful as my hands. And she wrestles with me for primacy, for her right to tip the bowl, spill the water all over the floor, and dump the food for the dogs to scavenge for it (because they, too, are wise to her moves and stand there in wait). All while I remain alert, trying not to be eviscerated.

Perhaps I need to learn to take the good with the bad and to accept that this might just be part of Graycie's way of reminding me—in case I'd forgotten—that wild birds usually don't want to be kept as pets. They want to soar through the atmosphere and enjoy their birdie lives as free creatures, even if it means being inhaled by a predator while sleeping in a tree one night after living only a few short months, rather than merely getting by while living in captivity for four or five (or nine!) decades. So when she latches on with intent to maim, I understand there is probably greater meaning to it. I don't appreciate it, but I do get it.

~~~~~~

One night not long ago as my family was eating dinner I looked over to see that Graycie was hanging over a branch looking particularly curious—her head was twisted around and cocked up, as if she was straining to hear our conversation, even though we were right there, perfectly within hearing distance. I pointed her pose out to the girls, who then started one of their favorite activities with her: clucking to get the bird dancing. Kendall and Gillian got up and went over to the tree and clucked again and again, flapping pretend wings, as Graycie clucked back, bobbing her body to the beat and cracking us up. So I guess sometimes she does like to be part of the family.

This occasion reminded me that soon these family vignettes will be a thing of the past; the kids will be grown and gone and the fleeting life moments recorded by our parrot won't include Kyle and the girls very much anymore. I realized I needed to treasure them as they happen, and try to forget about Graycie's vicious streak, and instead appreciate her as being part of our family, which for any family member requires accepting their best and their worst traits.

CHAPTER 25

The Yin and Yang of Graycie

We've had our sad moments with pets over the years, putting down both Hobbes and Mink, who lived to be twenty and twenty-two, respectively. And, of course, Beau. Their memories live on, however, whenever Graycie calls out their names and we are reminded of them yet again.

In a way Graycie is to us like Kilroy during World War II, or more like our very own Forrest Gump: many high points of our lives, and many of the mundane moments, as well, have been crystallized in time through her utterances. She is our touchstone.

She is also a pain in the behind. I cannot sit down to relax in the living room for even thirty seconds without her reminding me that she is there and wants me to know it. If she is on the cage, she will immediately begin to plink the bars, insisting that I acknowledge her presence. She won't do this for the kids, who can spend hours lounging in the living room watching television. But send me in there exhausted and needing a moment's peace, and she's like a fourth-grade boy waiting to dip a little girl's pigtails in the inkwell.

On a recent night she wasn't content with simply plinking. Instead she grew silent. And then I heard her say out loud, "Jenny!"

The sound came from an unfamiliar quadrant of the room. We are all so used to her voice coming at us from the corner in which she resides that it's jarring to hear it from anywhere else. I got up to search and found her in her favorite spot, by the parrot cabinet. She was standing in front of the cabinet, trying to open it up. For fun, because I had the time to actually supervise her, I decided to open the cabinet and let her have at it. So for a good forty minutes she happily hung out, pulling down little wooden blocks and toys and an old sock stuffed with pieces of wood and all the while talking, talking, talking.

Like the child who has the time of his life at Chuck E. Cheese then throws himself on the ground in a fit of fury when it's time to leave, Grayce was unwilling to leave her playland as bedtime approached. Once her belligerence kicked in, this time, unlike so many others, I was wise: I slapped on two pairs of protective gloves—the most durable ones I could find at the hardware store short of the chain mail variety—and was able to get her on the wooden perch. I hastened her over to the cage, but she refused to go inside. It was late and I was tired. I tried to lure her the usual ways, first with food, then with fingers. As I tried to close the top of the cage, she got me. Despite the sturdy gloves, she still managed to break a blood vessel in my hand, leaving a lovely dark bruise behind. Once again, the pleasure of watching her enjoy some modicum of freedom was eclipsed by the pain of caring for a thankless pet. She's always keeping me on my toes.

~~~~~

We recently celebrated Mia and Keith's golden anniversary—Scott and I, our kids, Mark and Laurie and their families—the whole parrot-loving group of us, in Costa Rica, where many parrots thrive in the wild, while others are kept like happy mistresses. There I realized with a pang of guilt that there are ways of captivity that are, if not desirable, at least somewhat palatable. As I watched Bert, a yellow-naped Amazon who lives at an open bar/restaurant in the tropical paradise of Playa Grande, I felt an even greater twinge of guilt that poor Graycie was at that moment home stuck in a cage, alone but for the petsitter.

Bert has a dream setup for a captive parrot: a five-foot-long tree branch as a perch suspended from the bar's roof overhang, with another long branch that extends diagonally to the ground to serve as a ramp, so he can go up and down at will, while the waitstaff provides him with leftovers that range from tropical fruits to filet mignon. Bert says "*hola*" to all the restaurant visitors, then climbs back diagonally to the top of his perch, shimmies over to a dangling ring suspended from the ceiling, and grabs on to it with his powerful claws and beak. Then a waiter takes the ring and whirls it about in a circle, the bird swirling faster and faster, releasing one foot and spinning happily, like a child on the Teacups at Disney World. Before you know it he's holding on with his beak, whipping around in a gleeful frenzy, the centrifugal force carrying the parrot away: "Look, Ma! No hands!" Bert seems like the happy drunk of the parrot world.

Elsewhere in Costa Rica we came upon a flock of domestic macaws being gradually introduced into the wild to help repopulate the area. We stared, transfixed, as the large, spectacularly brilliant scarlet, blue, and gold colored parrots fought with one another for primacy in the crook of a tree. Others nestled together on stoops, free to come and go as they pleased. And still others took off at will, rainbows in flight. They had the best of both birdie worlds.

This made me feel very sad for Graycie on one level: that she was deprived of the chance for freedom seems so cruel. She was never given much of a chance to spread her powerful wings and take flight, or to simply pluck a ripe mango from a tree, or to fly en masse amid a cloud of gray and red cohorts. I feel exceptionally guilty when Graycie stretches her wings out, because they actually creak when she does this. It reminds me of the Tin Man, unable to move well due to disuse. When Graycie stretches, she does it one wing at a time, stretching as far as her extended wing will go, reaching the same side leg out as well and pointing her foot gracefully, holding the pose like a bodybuilder for ten seconds or so. It's a beautiful gesture.

~~~~~

The other night Scott, the kids, and I sat down and watched some home videos. Throughout, in the background of much of our children's childhoods, were interspersed comments by Graycie. To hear it in hindsight like that was particularly charming and made me realize that she is such an integral part of our lives.

Gillian, who must've also picked up on Graycie's unique place in our family, said, "You know, Mom, Graycie's sort of sad as a teenager because usually teens have these really important dates highlighting special occasions: their sixteenth birthday, they can drive; they turn eighteen, they go to college. But for poor Graycie, it's nothing but the same old thing." For Graycie, no matter what we've done to spice things up, her days must run together in an endless stream of boredom.

We are nearing an important crossroads: a son almost halfway through college, a daughter just months away from leaving for university, and the youngest daughter who in two short years will also move onward. We've spent so many years readying these kids to fly, encouraging and sometimes forcing them from the nest so that they could become whatever they choose to become, and flourish as adults. And yet we will still have that black-beaked child reminding us so often of days that have become but memories of another time in life.

~~~~~

The kids—and the bird, for that matter—have taught us volumes about patience, about letting the course of life fall into place, and about loving and understanding and realizing that you can no more make your child fit a mold you think is the one for them than can you turn a wild parrot into a docile house pet. And Graycie has taught our kids plenty. For one thing, Kyle learned that he never wants to own a parrot. He can't abide the endless noise from the bird or the dogs, for that matter; sort of like a child subjected to his parents' cigarette smoke, he rejects the bad habit. But Graycie has taught them all to nurture: she's taught them tolerance. She's taught them the importance of sticking out hard times. She has been the bearer of life lessons we'd have never guessed a small bird could carry with her. In her own inimitable (ironic, for a creature that imitates by nature) way.

On the flip side, she's been spared the unenviable experience of slipping slowly down the constrictive gullet of a hungry snake, or swooped upon by a much larger eagle, plucked from a tree branch, and ultimately torn into bite-size bits for the raptor's eaglets.

I guess when you hash it all out, Graycie could've had it worse. As could we.

CHAPTER 26

Bird *Not* for Sale

If this memoir has *still* left you wondering why we put up with Graycie's downsides, despite having not quite as many evident upsides, well, I suppose you wouldn't be the only one. The short answer is, I guess you'd have to live with Graycie to really understand it. But aside from that nebulous notion, Scott and I have always been of the mind-set that when you make a commitment to raise a pet, you stick with it. Quitting isn't in our repertoire. At least not when it comes to other living, breathing creatures. Even if they are surlier than your average rabid raccoon, and even if we didn't exactly make the commitment directly out of the box, and rather the thing showed up on our doorstep and turned into the gift that keeps on giving. But how could we turn her away, all gangly and fuzzy and quaking on her perch?

Ours is a fish out of water—make that bird out of jungle—story about two very divergent types of creatures thrown together by fate, thoroughly ill equipped to deal with each other and forced to make the best of a challenging situation. And

· 235

through the arc of our lengthy relationship with Graycie, Scott and I have truly learned—and imparted to our children—that agreeing to care for an animal isn't a quid pro quo as long as it all works out swimmingly. The message we've sent to our kids and the one that is our mantra is *You make a commitment to a living thing for life.*

We've come to love our peculiar little gray friend, despite her propensity toward violence. And while I may often remind her that she'd probably have ended up being eaten alive by a green mamba just like the parrot in *The Poisonwood Bible* had she stayed in Zaire, the fact is, our lives are all the richer for having shared twenty years with our curmudgeonly African gray.

I can't say that I love her in that cuddly baby puppy sort of way. But I'm so darned *accustomed* to her. We've been through so much together, and as much as I struggle to admit this at times, I'd miss the bird if she weren't there every day, making her presence known. I'd miss the jungle screechings on those rare rainy afternoons when I'm trying to nap (maybe). I'd miss the obsessive-compulsive cage thrumming. I'd miss the constant challenge of avoiding the malicious intentions of one fast-as-lightning, nutcracker-beaked, beady-eyed hellion. I'd miss her yelling at my dog who's been dead for a decade, warning her to not track mud in the house. I'd miss her shrill mimicry of the smoke detector chirp, the one that goes off every sixty seconds as the battery dies, and I'd certainly miss her asking my once one-year-old daughter, now headed off to college, if she wants more strawberries.

I'm about to become an empty-nester, but for one family member who actually builds nests. So the parrot who became part of the family right when Scott and I began our family will be the remaining legacy at home with us, constantly taking us back to snapshots of our lives with children: calling out for Gillian, yelling "Hey, Kyle!," offering up fruit to Kendall, and still putting our kids in time-outs, maybe even when they have become parents themselves and have their own children to put in time-out.

And maybe once all the kids are gone in just a couple of years, instead of laughing when she does this I'll cry, mournful for the days gone by.

I suppose when that day comes we'll finally have time to really devote to Graycie. We used to think we had all the time in the world: when Graycie first came home, the common belief was that African grays could live to be eighty years old. But not long ago, our new parrot vet told us she's rarely seen a gray live past forty years, in captivity. So with some luck (or not, depending on how you see it), we'll still have half her life left in which to finally persuade Graycie that we're friend, not foe.

We started out this journey with a dog, two cats, and a newborn. And then Graycie flapped into our lives. We've raised our three children, said goodbye to three pets, and now we find ourselves almost back at the beginning. No more kids at home, but a bird, to whom I can devote much more attention, but whom I still can't trust to not eviscerate me, given the opportunity. It's just us now, but it won't be quiet, not with a squawking, talking parrot around, one who loves to make sure she's not forgotten in the fray.

~~~~~~

It's been reported that Henry VIII owned an African gray parrot. I'm willing to bet that right next to the large guillotine used to dispense with his uncooperative wives was a miniature version with which he beheaded his parrot. No man with such thin patience could otherwise deal with a bird so much cleverer than he. Trust me, on more than one occasion I've longed for my very own birdie guillotine.

Although to be fair, maybe he'd have killed off more wives without the amusing diversions of his clever parrot. Certainly for us there are those golden moments with our parrot that brighten our mood, and for that, I am grateful. And despite the power of nature over nurture, we have been able to relish those brief periods of time in which we've managed to breach the species divide, that one that keeps us from ever being fully trusting of Graycie and her of us. And when I finish singing Graycie her bedtime song and give her a big fat air kiss, and she makes a loud smacking kiss sound and says, "Good night! I love you!," it's a moment when we've made a connection, and it justifies all of our hard-fought efforts (and hers, for that matter) to come to that meeting point.

We walk a tenuous tightrope, only occasionally connecting as fellow travelers on this planet, but when we do, in those moments when she offers up her head for us to pet, it's especially gratifying. Then, we're no longer rivals, just family.

Epilogue

After I completed this manuscript, I stumbled upon Matt Smith from Project Perry (www.projectperry.com), a parrot rescue sanctuary that just happens to be near me. I'd seen a snippet of something on the local news that showed images of African grays, so I followed up to find out what it was about.

Matt began working in parrot rescue after losing a parrot to disease shortly after he'd brought him home from a pet store, as a way to work through the grief of losing a beloved pet. This led to Project Perry, which is often involved in uncovering parrot breeding mills and rescuing parrots from these cruel and unhealthful situations (last year their group rescued thirty-one tragically abused macaws from squalid conditions at a breeder's). Project Perry's aviary is also a way station for parrots whose owners realize too late that parrots are a *lot* of work, parrots who outlive their owners, and even parrots whose owners find partners who don't want to deal with a bird.

Last summer Project Perry put the final touches on an exquisite indoor/outdoor African gray sanctuary, in which now are housed some twenty African grays who were salvaged from tortured lives in squalid quarters not much bigger than a bread box and forced to breed their entire adult lives. Matt has made me aware of the existence of this parrot mill culture, which is pretty rampant in the United States—unsavory breeders can make a lot of money selling parrots to unsuspecting customers. Seeing the menagerie of African grays flying near-freely within their new aviary home was sobering for me, because I knew how much Graycie would love to be able to move freely from tree to tree, to socialize with birds of her ilk, and to not be closed into her cage, no matter how generously sized it might be.

If you are going to consider adopting a parrot, please do your research, and try to ensure that you are purchasing a parrot from a reputable breeder. Or better yet, consider adopting a parrot from one of several parrot rescue organizations in the United States. The folks at Project Perry would be happy to help you find a rescuer near you. Please visit www.project perry.com for further information.

Acknowledgments

With deepest gratitude, I'd like to thank the following people whose help in ushering this memoir to publication was invaluable: My fabulous agent, Holly Root, who championed Graycie's story even though birds sorta scare the crap out of her; my equally fabulous editor Emily Westlake (who just knew Graycie had a charming side); Jennifer Bergstrom and the entire team at Gallery who believed in this book; Wade Rouse, Kristy Kiernan, and my Debutante Ball sisters for generously reading the memoir and providing lovely quotes; Michelle McConnell, Claire Harrelson, Sonjia Smith, and Suzanne Macpherson, who are always willing to find time to do early reads and provide input; my wonderful family (hope you don't mind, you've formally been outed); and to the many kind readers who have taken the time to e-mail me and whose positive feedback has encouraged me to keep writing. Lastly, thanks to dear friends Gary and Tana Taylor, Kelley and Eric Johnson and Liz and Bill Estep, for your perpetual support and being such great vacation buddies.

About the Author

Jenny Gardiner, author of the award-winning novel *Sleeping with Ward Cleaver,* lives in Virginia with her husband, three children, and a menagerie of demanding pets. She loves to hear from readers, so please visit her at www.jennygardiner.net, http://twitter.com/jennygardiner and http://www.facebook.com/jenny.gardiner.